THE US–JAPAN ALLIANCE IN THE 21ST CENTURY:

A VIEW OF THE HISTORY AND A RATIONALE
FOR ITS SURVIVAL

JDS *Yugumo.*

THE US–JAPAN ALLIANCE IN THE 21ST CENTURY

A VIEW OF THE HISTORY
AND A RATIONALE FOR ITS SURVIVAL

by

FUMIO OTA

**GLOBAL
ORIENTAL**

THE US–JAPAN ALLIANCE IN THE 21ST CENTURY
A VIEW OF THE HISTORY AND A RATIONALE FOR ITS SURVIVAL

First published in English 2006 by
GLOBAL ORIENTAL LTD
PO Box 219
Folkestone
Kent CT20 2WP
UK

www.globaloriental.co.uk

ISBN 1-905246-25-0
ISBN 978-1-905246-25-0 [13-digit]

British Library Cataloguing in Publication Data
A CIP catalogue entry for this book is available from the British Library

Set in 10/12pt Stone Serif by Servis Filmsetting Ltd, Manchester
Printed and bound in England by Athenaeum Press, Gateshead, Tyne & Wear

Contents

Foreword

For more than half a century the United States and Japan have been working together to secure common interests. Crafted during the beginning of the Cold War as Japan was in post-war ruin, both nations deliberately and completely changed their relationship from enemies to allies on September 8, 1951, concluding the San Francisco Peace Treaty, and on the same day signing the Treaty of Mutual Cooperation and Security which went into effect in 1952. Since that day, the US and Japan have squarely addressed major security concerns and worked toward common objectives.

The alliance has endured decades as the security mainstay for both countries in East Asia, however, there has been absolutely nothing stagnant about it. One obvious example is the 1960 revision of the Treaty of Mutual Cooperation and Security which gave Japan greater voice in the stationing of US troops. Since its inception, Japan has become an economic superpower with far-reaching global interests; we have successfully put the Cold War behind us; and Japan now deploys its own forces around the globe in support of peace-keeping and disaster-relief operations. It is no wonder that the endurance of the US-Japan alliance and its endurance through changes in the security environment draws the attention of scholars.

Admiral Fumio Ota is one who offers a unique perspective with keen insights into the relationship. Studying alliance relationships in a language other than his mother-tongue, Admiral Ota outlines comparisons and provides his analysis of the alliance. His personal experiences serving in the

Japanese Maritime Self-Defense Force (JMSDF) are very much a part of this work.

Admiral Ota explains the spirit of exceptionally close navy-to-navy cooperation between the JMSDF and US Navy, and their role in the alliance. He does this by providing first-hand accounts of when he commanded the JDS *Yugumo* during missions in Northeast Asia. Furthermore, he provides accounts of situations when he served as the Defense Attaché to the US, and cases of US-Japan intelligence cooperation as Director of Japan's Defense Intelligence Agency. This includes US assistance in non-combatant evacuation operations in Albania, Estonia, and Sierra Leone, and areas where US support of JSDF deployments have contributed to mutual successes. Through these accounts he demonstrates that the security relationship is truly a global one. His service in the operational, policy, and intelligence arenas of the alliance provides a rare glimpse into the operations of those who work within the alliance day-to-day.

Admiral Ota rightfully notes the imbalance of the security arrangement. These include areas where the US commits to the defense of Japan and territories under its administration without the reciprocal commitment on the part of Tokyo, and how Japan's prohibition of collective self-defense constrains alliance cooperation. He recognizes that much of the alliance's success is due to its foundation based on mutual national interests and offers his views on how this security arrangement can be further strengthened.

Richard L. Armitage
Former US Deputy Secretary of State

Preface

The year 2004 was the 150th anniversary of the Treaty of Kanagawa – the first treaty of peace and amity between the United States and Japan.

We can divide these 150 years into three phases of approximately 50 years each. First, from the Treaty of Kanagawa in 1854 to the Russo-Japanese War in 1904–05, the relationship between the US and Japan was relatively friendly, as exemplified by President Theodore Roosevelt's support for Japan during the Russo-Japanese War.

The second phase was from the Treaty of Portsmouth (the outcome of the Russo-Japanese War) in 1905 to 1952 (when the Treaty of Peace with Japan and the US–Japan Security Treaty entered into force), the US–Japan relationship became unfriendly, then subsequently unsustainable and ultimately ended in war triggered by Japan's attack on Pearl Harbor in 1941.

In the third phase, from 1952 up to the present, the US and Japan have enjoyed a strong and stable alliance. The question is, what will be the relationship between the two parties for the next 50 years? This volume will endeavor to answer this fundamental question by reviewing history to determine what factors make alliances, and what factors cause them to break down or disintegrate; furthermore, the question of alliance rationale for the US, Japan and the region as a whole is also considered.

Through close analysis of the current issues supported by various case studies, we can conclude that in the 21st century, a continuing sound alliance, based on an interdependent relationship between the US and Japan, will ensure the future stability of the Asia Pacific region.

FUMIO OTA

1

Alliance Rationale Theory

Classic alliance theories have always been based on power and threat. In 1814, Metternich stated: 'Alliances . . . [like] all fraternization, if they do not have a strictly determinate aim, . . . disintegrate.'[1] The great international relations theorist, Hans J. Morgenthau stated:

> Alliance is a necessary function of the balance of power operating within a multiple-state system. Nations A and B, competing with each other, have three choices in order to maintain and improve their relative power positions. They can increase their own power, they can add to their own power the power of other nations, or they can withhold the power of their nations from the adversary. When they make the first choice, they embark upon an armaments race. When they choose the second and third alternatives, they pursue a policy of alliances.[2]

Kenneth N. Waltz wrote:

> States will ally with the devil to avoid the hell of military defeat. . . . As soon as someone looks like the winner, nearly all jump on the bandwagon rather than continuing to build coalitions intended to prevent anyone from winning the prize of power. Bandwagoning, not balancing, becomes the characteristic behavior.[3]

He also argued in his article *The Emerging Structure of International Politics*:

. . . for a country to choose not to become a great power is a structural anomaly. For that reason, the choice is a difficult one to sustain. . . . Japanese and German reasons for hesitating to take the final step into the great-power arena are obvious and need not be rehearsed. . . . How long can Japan and Germany live alongside other nuclear states while denying themselves similar capabilities? . . . Japanese and German nuclear inhibitions arising from World War II will not last indefinitely; one might expect them to expire as generational memories fade.[4]

Stephen M. Walt stated:

When confronted by a significant external threat, states may either balance or bandwagon. *Balancing* is defined as allying with others against the prevailing threat; *Bandwagoning* refers to alignment with the source of danger. Thus, two distinct hypotheses about how states will select their alliance partners can be identified on the basis of whether the states ally against or with the principal external threat.[5]

K.J. Holsti wrote:

When two or more parties perceive a common threat, they are likely to engage in various types of military collaboration, which can range from the informal provision of technical advisers, granting of arms, or exchange of information, to its most concrete form: a formal alliance.[6]

In his article *Back to the Future: Instability in Europe After the Cold War*, John J. Mearsheimer argued: 'It is the Soviet threat that provides the glue that holds NATO together. Take away that offensive threat and the United States is likely to abandon the Continent, whereupon the defensive alliance it has headed for forty years may disintegrate'.[7] However, the reality is that, six years after Mearsheimer wrote this, NATO is still alive.

In *When Trust Breaks Down*, Charles W. Kegley, Jr. and Gregory A. Raymond stated: 'A cardinal principle of balance-of-power theory is that alliances formed prior to or during wartime to combat a common adversary will disintegrate when the common enemy is defeated.'[8] A typical example of this principle is the relationship between the US and the Soviet Union during and after World War II.

After the Cold War, two phenomena have occurred. First, the Soviet Union and the Warsaw Pact dissolved. Second, in contravention, alliances with the US, such as NATO and the bilateral alliances of the Asia-Pacific region, have been enlarged or strengthened despite the demise of the common threat, the Soviet Union.

NATO's Strategic Concept, approved by the Heads of State and Governments participating in the meeting of the North Atlantic Council in Washington DC on April 23 and 24, 1999, stated that NATO has played an essential part in strengthening Euro-Atlantic security since the end of the Cold War.[9] The Czech Republic, Poland and Hungary were invited to join NATO in April 1999. NATO made the second expansion by inviting seven new countries to join the Alliance in March 2004: Bulgaria, Estonia, Latvia, Lithuania, Romania, Slovakia and Slovenia. The third expansion will be possible including Albania, Croatia and Macedonia. Immediately after the 11 September terrorist attack on the US, NATO agreed to execute Article 5 of the Atlantic Treaty – to conduct collective defense. This is the first time NATO has invoked this right of collective defense since its establishment in 1949. In February 2002, US Deputy Secretary of Defense, Paul Wolfowitz made the following remarks at the Munich Conference on European Security Policy:

> Ten years ago, during the Cold War, many people – on both sides of the Atlantic – said that we didn't need NATO any more. Some said that the threat had gone away. Others said that American's involvement in European security was no longer needed. Yet ten years later, NATO continues to be the key to security and stability in Europe, most notably in the Balkans, where, as President Bush said in Warsaw last June, 'we went in . . . together, and we will come out together.' and now, for the first time in its history, NATO has involved Article V, not because of an attack on Europe, but because the United States itself has been attacked by terrorists operating from abroad.[10]

In the Declaration by Heads of State and Government of NATO Member States and the Russian Federation issued on 28, May 2002, stated that the member states of the North Atlantic

Treaty Organization and the Russian Federation are today opening a new page in our relations, aimed at enhancing our ability to work together in areas of common interest and to stand together against common threats and risks to our security.[11]

The United States Security Strategy for the East Asia-Pacific Region – the so-called Nye initiative, in 1995[12] and the second version in 1998[13] – has strengthened Asia-Pacific alliances for the East Asia-Pacific Region. *A National Security Strategy for a New Century*, published by the White House in December 1999, stated that: '. . . our continuing security role is further reinforced by our bilateral alliances with the Republic of Korea, Australia, Thailand, and the Philippines'.[14] *The United States and Asia: Toward a New US Strategy and Force Posture* published by the Rand Corporation, stated:

> Knitting together a coherent web of security arrangements among the United States and its core partners in Asia – Japan, Australia and South Korea – that might expand to Southeast Asia will demand military as well as political steps. Training exercises will need to be expanded to include all the parties; planning forums will need to be established; and some degree of hardware standardization will be necessary to foster human and technical interoperability. Particularly useful in this regard could be the deployment of procedures and mechanisms for greater information sharing between the United States and its core regional partners at the strategic, operational, and tactical levels.[15]

This is such an important concept to the United States, that the title of chapter III in *The National Security Strategy of the United States of America* published in September 2002 is 'Strengthen Alliance to Defeat Global Terrorism and Work to Prevent Attacks Against Us and Our Friends'.[16]

The US–Japan alliance was reaffirmed through the Joint Declaration between President Clinton and Prime Minister Hashimoto in April 1996 which was followed by the new Guidelines for Japan-US Cooperation Review in 1997 and the Ballistic Missile Defense (BMD) co-research direction agreement in 1998. The new Guidelines for Japan-US Cooperation concertedly and precisely defined what Japanese Self-Defense Forces would do during a crisis, whereas the old Guidelines provided only a framework for coordination. Also, the new

Guidelines focus on cooperation in response to regional contingencies, while the old Guidelines focused more narrowly on the direct defense of Japan. In August 1999, US and Japan exchanged the official documents and signed the Memorandum of Understanding between the Governments of Japan and the US on Japan-US Cooperative Research on Ballistic Missile Defense. Defense Agency Director-General Yoshinori Ono and US Ambassador Howard Baker signed the Missile Defense Agreement in December 2004, a week after Japan ended its decades-old ban on military exports (but only to the United States for the defense system). Under the memorandum of understanding, Japan and the United States will form a committee to share information and do away with the lengthy paperwork for the research. In December 2004, the Japanese Security Council and the Cabinet approved the National Defense Program Guideline for FY 2005 and After, which stated the Japan-US Security Arrangements are indispensable for Japan's security.[17]

The Acquisition and Cross-Servicing Agreement (ACSA), which permits US Forces and the Japanese Self-Defense Force to exchange logistic support items and services, continues to evolve. In 1996, the ACSA could only be used during combined exercises. The ACSA was expanded in 1999 to permit exchanges during Situations In Areas Surrounding Japan (SIASJ). After the so-called anti-terrorism legislation passed the Diet in October 2001, the ACSA applied not only to SIASJ, but also to any area in the world except combatant zones. Furthermore, it expands to not only US Forces, but also to other nations' armed forces. Today, Japan Maritime Self-Defense Force oilers have supplied US Naval combatants about 40 percent of the total fuel requirements during Operation Enduring Freedom under the Japanese special legislation for anti-terrorism. Finally, with the new Emergency Law passed the Diet in June 2003, the US Ambassador in Tokyo and the Japanese Minister of Foreign Affairs signed the so-called wartime ACSA in February 2004. The bilateral ACSA Procedural Agreement (PA) was signed on 15 July 2004 and ratified by the Diet with an effective date of 31 July 2004. These developments continue and serve to illustrate the strengthening of the US–Japan alliance in the area of bilateral military cooperation.

The Japanese Joint Staff Office (JSO) and the US Pacific

Command agreed to exchange officers in 2000. JSO dispatched liaison officers to the US Central Command in Florida after the September 11, 2001 terrorist attack on the US, and also send several liaison officers to the Multinational Force-Iraq in Baghdad after the Self-Defense Force deployment. These actions provide further evidence of a strong and robust alliance.

When the USS *Kitty Hawk* got underway from Yokosuka after the September 11 attack on the US, Japan Maritime Self-Defense Force (JMSDF) ships accompanied her. Ships from the Japan Coast Guard's also escorted the *Kitty Hawk* with armed personnel on board, and the Ministry of Land, Infrastructure and Transport prohibited the flying of civilian aircraft around the American aircraft carrier. After the so-called anti-terrorism legislation passed the Diet in October 2001, the JMSDF dispatched several ships to the North Arabian Sea while Japan Air Self-Defense Force (JASDF) C-130 aircraft airlifted American soldiers from Japan to South East Asia on several occasions. In December 2002, the Japanese Government finally decided to dispatch the AEGIS destroyer *Kirishima*. These kinds of cooperative actions are firsts since the US–Japan alliance was established in 1951. President Bush spoke to the Japanese Diet on February 18, 2002 and said: 'The Japanese response to the terrorist threat has demonstrated the strength of our alliance.'[18]

Charles W. Kegley, Jr., and Gregory A. Raymond also stated in their book, *When Trust Breaks Down*:

> Throughout history, where there has been rivalry between great powers, there has also been mistrust and misperception. The two giants' manifest and latent power fueled their fears of each other. These fears were compounded by cognizance of the new areas in which their interests came into conflict, and were animated by the suspicions that inevitably accompany the withering away of old arrangements in the face of new realities.[19]

At least in an economic sense, the US and Japan are giants, because their total GDP is about 45 percent of the world's GDP. However, the two nations have not come into conflict, but instead continue to strengthen their alliance. Why?

The American Quadrennial Defense Review (QDR), published in September 2001, established a new paragraph, *Strengthening Alliances and Partnerships* in Defense Strategy, which was not seen in the old QDR of May 1997.[20] As far as other US security alliances in the Pacific, the 28th Republic of Korea (ROK)-US Security Consultative Meeting Joint Communiqué stated: '. . . the ROK-US long-term security relationship should continue to be developed in a mutually beneficial way'.[21] The trilateral security talks among Japan, the US, and ROK have been dramatically enhanced since the late 1990s. Even though Japan and the ROK are not formally allied because of historic animosity rooted in the early 1900s, Tokyo and Seoul agreed that the ROK would gradually open its doors to Japanese popular culture, including music, drama and films. Security ties have grown and there have been an exchange of visits by the respective defense ministers, as well as student exchanges, ship port calls and the opening of hotlines. The first Japan-ROK joint naval search-and-rescue exercise was held in August 1999. Retired US Air Force Colonel Ralph A. Cossa of the Pacific Forum Center for Strategic & International Studies (CSIS) stated that US, Japan, and Korea are creating a 'Virtual Alliance'.[22] Japan Ground Self-Defense Forces and the Korean Army worked side by side in East Timor in 2003.

The security relationship between the US and Australia was also strengthened by a Joint Security Declaration, the so-called Sydney Statement of 1996[23] and the Joint Communiqué in 1997. The Sydney Statement announced intentions to expand joint military training exercises and reaffirm their commitment to long-term continuation of common signal intelligence sites in Australia in the future.[24] President Clinton during a visit to Canberra in November 1996, made a speech at Parliament in which he stated: '. . . the US-Australian relationship is the strongest we have ever had . . . Our alliance is not for only present time but must endure.'[25] The first item in the Joint Communiqué was to further strengthen and advance the US-Australia alliance relationship.[26] In March 1997, TANDEM THRUST, a combined US-Australia force-on-force field training exercise, was the largest military exercise conducted in Australia since World War II. Some 17,000 US and 5,000 Australian troops participated.[27] President Clinton addressed to Australian Parliament, in October 1997: 'The defense links between the United States and Australia have never been stronger . . . Today I say, again, with utter confidence, our alliance is not just for this time, it is for all time.'[28] The US Secretary of Defense, Donald H. Rumsfeld and Secretary of State, Colin Powell visited

Australia in July 2001 and talked with Australian Minister of Defense, Peter Reith, and Minister of Foreign Affairs, Alexander Downer. They agreed to enhance mutual accommodation between the US and Australian Armed Forces.

Furthermore, the US, Japan and Australia have developed another trilateral security relationship. During the ASEAN Regional Forum (ARF) held in Hanoi, Vietnam in July 2001, Australian Minister for Foreign Affairs, Alexander Downer proposed to Japanese Minister of Foreign Affairs, Makiko Tanaka the trilateral security framework to discuss Asian security issues. After the September 11 terrorist attack on the US, Australia also executed Article 5 of the Australia, New Zealand and the United States (ANZUS) Treaty – to conduct collective defense. This is the first time an ANZUS signatory has invoked this right of collective defense since its establishment in 1951. Secretary of State, Colin L. Powell testified at a budget hearing before the Senate Foreign Relations Committee on February 5, 2002 and stated: 'we also reinvigorated our bilateral alliances with Japan, Korea and Australia'.[29]

Although Singapore has no formal alliance with the US, the government announced in early 1998 that its Changi Naval Station, which became operational in the year 2000, would be available to US naval combatants and would include a pier to accommodate American aircraft carriers. To this end, the USS *Kitty Hawk* moored at Changi in April 2001. Additionally, the US and Singapore agreed to an ACSA in April 2000.

In January 1998, the US and the Republic of the Philippines negotiated a Visiting Forces Agreement, which was ratified in May 1999. This agreement permits routine combined exercises and training, and ship visits.[30] A total of 5000 US and Philippine soldiers and sailors conducted a joint exercise, named *Balikatan* 2000, from January to March 2000. Bilateral exercises between the US and the Philippines have taken place since 1995. *Balikatan* was also conducted from April to May in 2001. In 2002, the US and the Philippines conducted *Balikatan* 2002 as Counter Terrorism Training (CTT) in the southern part of the Philippines from January to June. Furthermore, Philippine and US defense authorities also established the Military Logistic Support Agreement (MLSA) in November 2002. Malaysia, which hitherto had been relatively anti-American, made an anti-terrorism agreement with the US in May 2002. In February 1999, the New Zealand Defense Minister Max Bradford visited the US, portending the end of more than a decade of chilly military relations.[31]

Why have alliances with the US been expanding and/or strengthening even after the demise of the threat from the Soviet Union? The purpose of this volume is to analyze this phenomenon and provide a rational theory to explain why the alliances have strengthened even after the threat has diminished.

Classic alliance theory cannot be used to explain these post-Cold War phenomena. They might, however, be explained in three ways: first, alliances are continuing because of their inertia; second, there are still threats such as North Korea or China in Asia; and third, most realists agree that the United States' dominant position makes it an attractive alliance partner and possible continued US benign primacy (economic and military) could extend bandwagon effects (i.e., tendency to associate with, rather than challenge, a hegemonic power).[32]

The inertia theory cannot explain those alliances with the US that have continued for more than ten years after the Cold War. Dana H. Allin observed that it seems to be enough to conclude that the largest reason for NATO to exist is inertia.[33] However, Kegley and Raymond argued in their book, *When Trust Breaks Down*: 'Though inertia may lengthen the life of an alliance, suspicion will grow when the common threat recedes.'[34] If remaining threats make alliances continue it cannot explain the growth of NATO nor the strengthening of US-Australian bilateral alliances. Even if the North Korean threat disappears, the US and the ROK have agreed publicly that the US-ROK alliance will continue.[35] The hegemony theory cannot explain why the US does not want to loose even one soldier during a crisis such as Kosovo. According to Huntington's works, the US is a reluctant superpower. One could argue that the true definition of hegemony must be applied to nations which seek to expand their power using military might, such as the Roman and Mongolian Empires. Additionally, US prestige was heavily damaged and the country was made vulnerable when the terrorist attack happened in September 2001. If the hegemony theory were true, alliances with the US would have weakened at that time. In reality, however, the alliances with the US were, in fact, strengthened.

Therefore, the strengthening alliances must be explained in

a different way using other cooperative rationale. The so-called theory of *Constructivism* or *theory of social construction* represented by Alexander Wendt, Peter Kantzenstein, and Martha Finnemore of Yale University provides one possible explanation. One *Constructivist*, Thomas Risse-Kappen began with the question: Why was it that a pattern of cooperation evolved in NATO that survived not only the ups and downs of the Cold War and various severe inter-allied conflicts, (from the 1956 Suez crisis to the conflict over Euromissiles in the 1980s) but also the end of the Cold War? Why is it that NATO has emerged as the strongest among the post-Cold War security institutions when compared to the Organization for Security and Cooperation in Europe (OSCE), or the West European Union (WEU), not to mention the EU's Common Foreign and Security Policy (CFSP)? [36] Risse-Kappen also wrote in his book *Cooperation Among Democracies*:

> Waltzian realism, for example, probably expects the gradual disintegration of the North Atlantic Alliance. The answer of traditional realism following Hans Morgenthau depends on scope conditions, namely the future of American power and of threats to European security. Liberal theory expects the persistence of the transatlantic security community and its extension to the new democracies in Eastern Europe and even to Russia, depending on the future of that country's transformation. But liberalism is indeterminate regarding the institutional form of this community. If one adds institutionalist arguments, though, a strong case emerges for the preservation of NATO. [37]

Thomas Risse-Kappen concluded that, 'traditional alliance theories based on realist thinking provide insufficient explanations of the origins, the interaction patterns, and the persistence of NATO. The North Atlantic Alliance represents an institutionalized pluralistic security community of liberal democracies.' [38] Risse-Kappen also stated in *Cooperation Among Democracies*:

> Finally, I draw policy conclusions for the future of the transatlantic relationship in a post-cold war environment. If the Western Alliance is based primarily on shared values, norms, and a collective identity rather than on the perception of a common threat, one should expect the transatlantic security community to persist in one institutional form or another. [39]

Risse-Kappen's analysis focused on only transatlantic alliances and not transpacific alliances. He also did not touch upon important current changes such as the development of the interdependent society or globalization. The post-Cold War alliance was driven not only by the threat, but also by other cooperative rationalizations, which include stability, interdependence, and globalism. This means that recent deeper economic and military interdependence and globalization have been making modern developed states so vulnerable that war among them will be of very low probability. Modern developed states' prosperity depends upon a stable international environment. These modern developed states share common interests for stability.

1.   STABILITY

Right after the end of the Cold War, three Navy Captains from Russia, the US, and Japan (myself) met at the Center for International Security and Arms Control at Stanford University, the co-director of which was former Secretary of Defense, Dr. William Perry. After four months of research, we produced a report entitled 'Naval Cooperation in the Pacific: Looking to the Future'. Our report analyzed each country's national interests, security concerns, security measures, and security proposals, and we presented several conclusions and recommendations. Regarding security concerns, we reached the conclusion – instability.[40]

Military organizations, which historically have been the most nationalistic, have become more transnational in character. Countries which do not feel threatened by their neighbors today, such as Canada, Australia, New Zealand, Scandinavia and Western Europe, all have military organizations which focus on transnational challenges such as Peace-Keeping Operations outside their countries. This is because their national interest is best served in a stable world which promotes their economic prosperity. The world has been shrinking, and economic interdependence has dramatically increased due to the transportation and information revolutions. Thus, national interests have shifted to global interests and the deterrence strategy of the Cold War era has become a stabilization strategy. In this sense, it is better to use the term *security relationship* rather than *alliance*. For example, even though Indonesia broke off the new Security Treaty with Australia due to the East Timor Independence issue in 1999, this treaty between Indonesia and Australia established in December 1995 was a new type of security relationship designed to pursue stability without any particular potential threat. Their desire is to contribute to regional security and stability in order to ensure circumstances in which their aspirations can be best realized for the economic development and prosperity of their own countries and the region.[41]

The US–Japan alliance was based on something more than just a common threat. If we look back through history at the relationship between the US and Japan since 1853 when Commodore Perry knocked on Japan's closed door, we would see that US–Japan relations were not always a wonderful one, especially after the Russo-Japanese War. We need only remember that the US–Japan security treaty was signed in 1951 at the same time as the Peace Treaty in San Francisco. America's incentive to make Japan an alliance partner was not only to counter the Sino-Soviet alliance of 1950, but to never again suffer a repeat of the severe fight in World War II. The alliance was designed to ensure that the US and Japan, who are the great powers on the East and West side of the Pacific Ocean, would never fight each other. This created stability in not only East Asia but also the whole Pacific region, regardless of how severe the US–Japan trade dispute would eventually become. Therefore, the US–Japan alliance was not threat-driven but stability-driven, so that even after the Cold War when instability factors persist, the alliance should remain strong and continue to be strengthened.

During the process of strengthening the US–Japan alliance, both official and unofficial voices in China heavily criticized the strengthening of this relationship. For example, *China's National Defense*, published in October 2000, stated:

> Some countries have continued to enlarge military blocs, strengthen military alliances and seek greater military superiority. . . . There are new negative developments in the security of the Asia-Pacific region. The United States is further strengthening its military presence and bilateral military alliances in this region, advocating the development of the TMD (Theater

Missile Defense) system and planning to deploy it in East Asia. Japan has passed a bill relating to measures in the event of a situation in the area surrounding Japan. All this goes against the tide of the times. Joint military exercises have increased in the region, to the detriment of trust between countries.[42]

China's National Defense in 2004, published in December 2004, also stated:

> The United States is realigning and reinforcing its military presence in this region by buttressing military alliances and acceleration deployment of missile defense systems. Japan is stepping up its constitutional overhaul, adjusting its military and security policies and developing the missile defense system for future deployment. It has also markedly increased military activities abroad.[43]

The Chinese logic is as follows (1) The Cold War is over (2) The foundation of the US–Japan alliance was the Soviet Union, which no longer exists and (3) The reason for strengthening the US–Japan alliance must be against a new threat, and that would be China. However, this view only looks at the US–Japan alliance in terms of classic, threat-based alliance theory. Chinese scholars and government officials usually complain that the bilateral alliance is old-fashioned and runs counter to the current peaceful international environment. However, China is still engaging in a bilateral relationship with North Korea, and signed the first friendship treaty with Russia in July 2001. Indeed, in the late 1970s and early 1980s, China was informally aligned with the US and Japan against the Soviet Union. Beijing actively encouraged the strengthening of the US–Japan alliance. Henry Kissinger stated: 'Either Mao Zedong or Zhou Enlai appreciated the US–Japan alliance when I visited China in 1972. Because it is easy for China to predict the Japanese political direction.' Clearly, this Chinese argument is not valid today. The US–Japan alliance does not make China an enemy, but rather encourages China to be a partner in the international community to better improve stability in the region.

The Japan-US Joint Declaration on Security Alliance for the 21st century, announced in April 1996, stated:

The Japan-US security relationship, based on the Treaty of Mutual Cooperation and Security between Japan and the United States of America, remains the cornerstone for achieving common security objectives, and for maintaining a stable and prosperous environment for the Asia-Pacific region as we enter the twenty-first century.[44]

National Defense Program Guideline for FY 2005 and After approved by the Japanese Security Council and the Cabinet on December 10, 2004 stated that the US military presence is critically important to peace and stability in the Asia-Pacific region, which continues to be stricken with unpredictability and uncertainty.[45]

In 1999 American and Japanese security alliance specialists, published *The US–Japan Alliance: Past, Present, and Future.* All of the authors – whether critics of the status quo or not – begin with the fundamental premise that the US–Japan alliance is critical to the maintenance of US interests and stability in the Asia-Pacific region.[46] Michael Mandelbaum stated in Foreign Affairs in 1991 that future dangers are nebulous and a nuclear-armed Japan will lead to insecurity; the US presence in East Asia is essential.[47]

The first items of the Sydney Statement, the Joint Security Declaration between Australia and the US of July 1996, was: promote democracy, economic development and prosperity, and strategic stability. As I stated before, *United States Security Strategy for the East Asia-Pacific Region 1998* advocates that the US-ROK alliance and military presence will continue to support stability both on the Korean Peninsula and throughout the region even after North Korea is no longer a threat.[48] The Japan-ROK-US 'virtual alliance' will provide stability in North East Asia after a unified Korea. A Chinese expert has even stated that continued US military presence in Korea after unification is a good idea. A researcher from the China Institute of International Strategic Studies (CIISS) further stated that US forces would 'serve as a buffer, a reassurance' against any armed animosity between Japan and Korea, although China would probably oppose 'the redeployment of US forces to the northern part of Korea close to the Chinese border'.[49] A Japanese specialist on Korean security, Narushige Michishita, wrote:

A Korea that is secure and anchored to the alliance is good not only for the relationship between Japan and Korea but also for the relationship between Korea and China. A secure Korea is likely to be less anti-Chinese and more interested in cooperation and bridge-building than an insecure Korea caught in the old geopolitical dilemma between two major powers . . . With the US forces presence in Korea, China and Korea would be inclined to moderate their behavior lest conflict escalate into a US-China confrontation. . . . A US presence in Korea could even stifle tension between Japan and China . . . Finally, without the maintenance of US forces in Korea, a US nuclear guarantee would ring hollow. By their presence, US forces would discourage Korea from developing a nuclear capacity, other weapons of mass destruction (WMDs) or offensive capabilities such as medium-range ballistic missiles. This, too, would have the effect of calming tensions between Japan and Korea, and between Korea and China.[50]

After the September 11 terrorist attack, the US began to create a global anti-terrorism network. Therefore, the US needs to make a coalition with old semi-hostile countries such as Russia and China. Importantly, the US–Japan alliance would have another role to check Russian and Chinese threats to other surrounding countries. This is yet another reason why a strengthened US–Japan alliance is good for regional stability.

The situation is the same in Europe. The US fought against Germany twice in the past. The present NATO framework provides a stable Europe. The NATO alliance prevents a power vacuum in Europe – a Germany without security ties to the US would bring back geostrategic insecurity on the continent.[51] After the end of the Cold War, instability factors such as Bosnia, Kosovo, and former Soviet satellites still exist. This is why NATO is still useful and is even enlarging. The London Declaration on a transformed North Atlantic Alliance issued by the heads of state and government of the North Atlantic Council in July 1990 stated: 'It can help build the structures of a more united continent, supporting security and stability with strength of our shared faith in democracy . . . '[52] The United States Security Strategy for Europe and NATO, published in 1995, stated: 'Building a new security architecture for Europe means providing a framework to build stable democracies, market economies, and ultimately a stable and just peace across the continent.'[53] The Madrid Declaration on Euro-Atlantic Security and Cooperation of July 1997 stated that improving the security and stability environments for nations in the Euro-Atlantic area where peace is fragile and instability currently prevails remains a major Alliance interest.[54] Dana H. Allin argued, 'the True purpose for NATO expansion is not to defend or threaten or attack against Russia but to expand political stability toward the east.'[55] *The Alliance Strategic Concept* also stated that the alliance has been at the heart of efforts to establish new patterns of cooperation and mutual understanding across the Euro-Atlantic region and has committed itself to essential new activities in the interest of a wider stability.[56] In fact, the situation in Kosovo was not a direct threat to the NATO countries, but instability resulting from such things as ethnic cleansing and refuge flows were. After the September 11 terrorist attack, NATO ministerials in December 2001 made a statement that the Alliance must adapt its capabilities to these changes in the conditions of security and stability.[57]

Thus, the US will never fight against other great powers, such as Germany, the UK and Japan, across the Pacific or the Atlantic. Those alliances create the stability, which transcend oceans.

Looking toward the future, the situation in Asia will be very complicated, indeed. Many unknown variables, such as the direction that China takes, the shape of a unified Korea, the probability of Russian resurgence, and the relationship among each of those states, increase uncertainty. If the US–Japan alliance remains firm, however, the options of those states to cause mischief will be very limited; thus, the stability in Asia will be maintained for the foreseeable future. Should the US remove its forces from Asia, each country in Asia would react by building up its own military capability – an arms race would surely begin. The ROK, for example, still fears Japanese aggression, especially if the US withdraws its forces from East Asia.[58] Therefore, the US military presence in the Asia-Pacific region is the guarantor for future regional stability. In the Strait of Taiwan crisis in March 1996, for example, the stock market in Hong Kong sharply declined, but recovered after the US sent two aircraft carriers to this area. During the defense summit talks of September 21, 1998, Fukushiro Nukaga, then the Director General of the Japan Defense Agency, stated that the reason why the Asian economic crisis did not become a security problem was because of the firm US–Japan alliance. William Cohen, former Secretary of Defense, also agreed with Mr Nukaga's opinion. When North and South Korean naval units exchanged fire on the west coast of Korea in June 1999, the conflict was deescalated only when the news that the US Seventh Fleet would deploy to the area was reported.

Richard J. Samuels and Christopher P. Twomey wrote:[59]

> If, in the absence of an alliance with the United States, Japan chose to aggressively balance against China, the region would face a dangerously destabilizing arms race. Korea and much of Southeast Asia would be forced to take sides. For Japan to truly compete in such a race, it would have to acquire nuclear weapons, a dangerous and destabilizing step that, in Harrison's words, 'would only provoke a more belligerent posture on the part of both China and Russia.'[60]

Moreover, while bilateral relations in which both sides possess secure second strikes is Japan to announce its development and possession of nuclear weapons. The same forces that lead China and Japan into an adversarial relationship in the first place might well push them to the brink of war. From a US perspective, this would be disastrous, for several reasons:

- War between two of America's largest trading partners would be devastating to the US economy.
- US involvement would be difficult: trying to avoid in a war between a former ally and a former enemy.
- War between a nuclear power and a threshold nuclear power would push the nuclear envelope in new and disconcerting ways.
- War between the two would be a humanitarian disaster.
- Nuclearization in Japan would press both Koreas to do the same, and perhaps pressure other Asian nations to follow suit.

The Quadrennial Defense Review (QDR) published in September 2001 stated in *Strengthening Alliances and Partnership*:

> As witnessed in the wake of the terrorist attacks on the United States, NATO's invocation of Article 5 demonstrates the commitment of America's partners to collective defense, which bolsters the security of the United States. These mutually reinforcing security relationships underpin the political stability on which the prosperity of civilized nations is built. And these arrangements are based on the recognition that a nation can be safe at home only if it is willing and able to contribute to effective security partnerships abroad.[61]

2.   INTERDEPENDENCE

Henry Kissinger, though deeply rooted in the classical tradition, has stated that:

> . . . the traditional agenda of international affairs – balance among major powers, security of nations – no longer defines our perils or our possibilities . . . Now we are entering a new era. Old international patterns are crumbling; old slogans are uninstructive; old solutions are unavailing. The world has become interdependent in economics, in communications, in human aspirations.[62]

We can discern key differences in alliances in the late-20th century from those that preceded them. Those early alliances were based on military cooperation – a temporary means of coalition and balancing. Alliances in the late-20th century began to embody values, becoming 'enduring alliances' characterized by political, economic, cultural and security institutions. This is yet another reason why the modern alliance will not disband easily, and is a key reason why Western alliances were strengthened, even as the Warsaw Pact dissolved after the Cold War. Thomas Risse-Kappen pointed out in his book *Cooperation Among Democracies*: 'Studying the former Warsaw Pact and comparing it to NATO appears to be problematic, since Soviet relations with Eastern Europe constituted an informal empire rather than an alliance among sovereign states.'[63]

British diplomat Robert Cooper sees there are three spheres in the world: (1) post-modern, characterized by matured freedom and a democratic political system, as well as a market economy; (2) pre-modern, without freedom nor democratic political system nor a market economy; and (3) modern, somewhere between post-modern and pre-modern.[64] Organization for Economic Cooperation and Development (OECD) countries, which belong in the post-modern sphere, are so interdependent and vulnerable that alliances among these countries have been enduring, despite the demise of threats against them. However, the alliances among countries in the modern and pre-modern sphere like the Warsaw Pact were easily dissolved after the Cold War.

For example, Article II in both NATO and the US–Japan Alliance refers to an economic collaboration. Article II in the Treaty of Mutual Cooperation and Security between Japan and the US states:

> The parties will contribute toward the further development of peaceful and friendly international relations by strengthening their free institutions, by bringing about a better understanding of the principles upon which these institutions are founded, and by promoting conditions of stability and well-being. They will seek to eliminate conflict in their international economic policies and will encourage economic collaboration between them.[65]

In 1990, immediately after the end of the Cold War, then US Ambassador to Japan, Mr Michael Armacost, made a speech at the National Institute for Defense Studies (NIDS) in Tokyo. As a student at NIDS then, I asked him about the possibility of changing the US–Japan Alliance after the Cold War. Ambassador Armacost immediately responded 'No, the US–Japan Alliance will not change even after the Cold War, because the alliance defines not only security relations but also political, economic, and cultural cooperation.'

Growing economic interdependence is one of the greatest characteristics in the modern world. According to Laura D'Andrea Tyson, who was President Clinton's Chairman of the Council of Economic Advisors, it is very difficult to ask which country is producing a certain good.[66] Today, for example, Toyota, GM, and VW design and produce a car together. During the late 1980s, Japan's Toshiba Machine Co. was accused by the US Government of breaching the rules of the Coordinating Committee for Export Control to Communist Area (COCOM) because it exported propellers for submarines to the Soviet Union. Even at that time though, the US was unable to make a clear legal case against Toshiba because so many American industries relied heavily on Toshiba's products. In Robert Cooper's post-modern sphere, countries are so interdependent that they become vulnerable to each other. Additionally, regarding the Toshiba incident, the interdependent relationship between the US Navy and the Japan Maritime Self Defense Force (JMSDF) solved the problem through such ways as building the Anti-Submarine Warfare (ASW) Center in Yokosuka. More recently, when a US submarine hit and sank the Japanese fishery training vessel, *Ehime Maru*, in February 2001, this close relationship between the US Navy and JMSDF again helped resolve a potentially major international incident. The JMSDF provided an Admiral for the US Navy's court of inquiry, as well as conferences with the affected local community. The JMSDF also sent divers and a submarine rescue vessel, JDS *Chihaya*, for the salvage operation. Therefore, the US Navy relied on the JMSDF to facilitate acquisition of Japanese cultural assets, as well as assist in cultural issues associated with a grieving local community. At last JDS *Chihaya* and its divers succeeded to ease victims' enmity.

Robert O. Keohane and Joseph S. Nye profiled other navy-to-navy examples in their book, *Power and Interdependence*:

> . . . transnational politics often takes place when complex inter-dependence conditions apply–in the monetary system when multiple channels of contact were greatest (the 1920s and 1960s) and in the oceans area since the late 1950s. Some transgovern-mental relations in oceans politics take place directly between governmental subunits. The British and American Navies regularly keep each other informed. Osgood reports that Indonesia and the United States have probably avoided a confrontation over straits by close Navy-to-Navy relations. Close Navy-to-Navy relations also helped prevent escalation in the Brazil-United States dispute over shrimp fishing in the early 1970s . . . All these cases indicate that some 'domestic' interests in the leading naval

power were not constrained by national boundaries in their choice of political strategies or coalition partners. [67]

As far as technology is concerned, the US and Japan depend heavily on each other. Under Secretary of Defense for Acquisition and Technology in the Clinton Administration, Dr Jacques S. Gansler, mentioned to me in October 1998 that when you open an American missile, you will find many Japanese computer chips. Japanese Self-Defense Forces also depend on US military technology. Following the end of the Cold War, defense budgets in many countries were reduced. In order to maintain affordable defense forces, mutual inter-dependence with allies and international cooperation are critically important. In fact, Japan and the US have developed many technical cooperative programs since 1980 when Dr William Perry, then-Under Secretary of Defense for Acquisition and Technology, created the *Systems and Technology Forum (S&TF)*. These include a Ducted Rocket Engine, a Crew Escape System, Advanced Hybrid Propulsion Technologies, Advanced Steel Technology, Fighting Vehicle Propulsion Technology Using Ceramic Materials, Cooperative Eye-safe Laser Radar Program, Shallow Water Acoustic Technologies, and Cooperative Ballistic Missile Defense Research. There are many successful examples of US–Japan technological cooperation. For example, Advanced Hybrid Propulsion Technologies combined Japan's strong point – production capability – with America's advantage in design. The US Navy had focused on deep water Anti-Submarine Warfare (ASW) during the Cold War era, whereas the Japan Maritime Self-Defense Force mainly operated in shallow water. Today, the US wants to obtain Japanese shallow water acoustic technology. US Navy combatants, including the post-Seawolf class submarines, the advanced destroyer, and future DDG-51 class destroyers, for example, will all use advanced steel technologies from Japan.

Gregg A. Rubinstein stated:

The past practice of separating sales and licensed production from technology development in US–Japan programs is no longer realistic. Equipment sales and R&D activities are not mutually exclusive, but increasingly interdependent.[68]

At the beginning of November 2001, the US Government finally approved production of the sophisticated AEGIS weapons system by four Japanese industries, Mitsubishi-Electronic, Mitsubishi-Heavy Industry, Oki, and NEC.

Robert Keohane and Joseph S. Nye argued in *Power and Interdependence* that 'Military interdependence has always existed, and military power is still important in world politics.'[69] This phenomenon of military interdependence and interoperability between allies was seen as early as after the Industrial Revolution. This is because the state that often launches a war cannot provide the resources and industries to sustain it without supplies from all over the world. Modern war requires a huge amount of ammunition and energy due to sophisticated weapons systems. Therefore, states tend to share not only their forces but also industrial powers as well as other resources. Even before the World War I, the continental countries' anti-French wars in the late 19th century were fought by the British financial supply. During the Franco-Prussian War in 1870, the new French military force was supplied by British equipment and supply. Japan fought the Russo-Japanese War mostly using foreign weapons and ammunitions. This concept extends technology to the idea of unified command as well. Norman Angell wrote *The Great Illusion* in 1912 and argued that war had now become impossible owing to the growing economic interconnectedness.[70] However, World War I soon broke out, rendering his theory void.

During World War I, allied headquarters under the command of French General Ferdinand Foch were established at the Western front in 1918. Though the war was almost over and this headquarters structure was both incomplete and limited, it was a good start on establishing international cooperation through combined military organization. One month after the Pearl Harbor attack, President Roosevelt and Prime Minister Churchill met with their military advisors at the Arcadia Conference in Washington to plan a coordinated effort against the Axis powers. At that time, the two Allied leaders established the Combined Chief of Staff (CCS) as the supreme military body for strategic direction of the Anglo-American war effort.[71] Then, after the World War II, NATO was established and exists to this day. Today, in the

Information Revolution age, technological and communications breakthroughs cross national borders so fast that those military institutions themselves become virtually borderless. Therefore, even after the demise of an overarching threat, post-modern sphere countries are so interdependent upon each other that they cannot go back to autonomous defense policies. Today, the degree of interdependence has become much deeper than before the World War I era when Norman Angell wrote *The Great Illusion*.

David S. Alberts, John J. Garstka, and Frederick P. Stein stated in their book *Network Centric Warfare*:

> Whether in traditional military engagements, asymmetrical engagements, or in a variety of operations other than war, the United States will be working in a coalition environment. Basic to the conduct of these operations is the ability to develop and maintain a shared perception of the situation, develop coherent plans that leverage the available resources, and execute them. This requires a level of information exchange, systems that can understand one another, a coalition-based planning process where all may participate, a common concept of operations, and a set of compatible procedures to carry out operations.[72]

Former US Naval War College President Vice Admiral Arthur K. Cebrowski stated in Tokyo in October 2000 that if you are not interoperable, then you are not on the net, not contributing, not benefiting, and not part of the information age.

This means that each country has abandoned a part of its national sovereignty. Autonomous defense policy is already the historic legacy of the previous age. *The Alliance's Strategic Concept* approved by NATO Heads of State and Government participating in the meeting of North Atlantic Council in Washington DC in April 1999 stated that member nations must be interoperable and have appropriate doctrine and technologies.[73] After the September 11 terrorist attack in the US, the relationship between Europe and the US has changed. During the 1990s, Europe had received considerable US help in meeting its security needs in places such as Bosnia and Kosovo, when European actions alone were insufficient. However, the US was attacked on its homeland on September 11, and could not respond to the crisis by itself. America needed its alliances' cooperation. This is because the world has become so interdependent.

Japan depends upon many national security factors, including uninterrupted access to oil, mineral resources, and food. Japan cannot survive without importing the above materials and currently does not have a strong enough naval capability to protect her Sea Lines Of Communication (SLOC). The US has the world's largest naval force and is the largest food supplier of Japan. However, in order to access and engage across the Asia-Pacific region, the US depends on its forward bases in Japan. In other words, Japan provides the strategic geographic location as well as the Host Nation Support, and the US in turn provides offensive military capabilities, including the nuclear umbrella. Moreover, regarding the naval forces, the Japan Maritime Self Defense Force does not possess the strike and power projection capability which the US Navy has, but it does possess strong Anti-Submarine and Mine Warfare capability of which the US Navy does not have enough. This complimentary, interdependent relationship has not changed following the Cold War but has, in fact become closer out of sheer necessity – the US Navy had almost 600 ships during the Cold War but it currently has a little over 300. Therefore, the US Navy is grateful to the JMSDF for dispatching several ships to the Arabian Sea for Operation Enduring Freedom. The Quadrennial Defense Review (QDR) of September 30, 2001, stated: 'Recent surveys conducted by the Department indicate that the two primary reasons that service members leave or consider leaving are basic pay and family separation . . . Family separation due to extended deployments has a significant impact on a family's propensity to remain in the military.'[74] JMSDF ship's participation reduces the US Naval ship's operational tempo and that helps to retain highly qualified people in the US Navy. This is another example of the intangible support relationships that the US–Japan military interdependency provides.

Ballistic Missile Defense cooperation between the US and Japan is a perfect example of military interdependence. In this case, an American Infrared Red (IR) sensing satellite could detect a hostile ballistic missile launch and transfer this real time to a JASDF Airborne Warning and Control System

(AWACS) E-3 aircraft, a JMSDF AEGIS destroyer and a Patriot missile battery. These defensive missile systems will then cover not only Japanese citizens but also US bases and personnel in Japan. If the JMSDF does not have enough AEGIS destroyers available, American AEGIS cruisers and destroyers stationed in around Japan could complement that capability. Neither the US nor Japan can defend itself without the other. Only defense cooperation effort makes it possible.

Dr Futoshi Shibayama in Aichi-Gakuin University presented a new concept in ballistic missile defense, Alliance Missile Defense (AMD), which can become an international missile defense arrangement for eliminating theater and strategic missile threats. He argued:

> As far as the US needs its allies' and Russia's participation in ballistic missile defense, Missile Defense (MD) or Ballistic Missile Defense (BMD) will not be appropriate concepts at all. After the US decided to abandon the Anti Ballistic Missile (ABM) Treaty, Theater Missile Defense (TMD) weapon systems of the next generation will shoot down ICBMs and SLBMs, so that a distinction between TMD and National Missile Defense (NMD) will eventually become meaningless.

In view of this future development, Dr Shibayama described major components of TMD in Japan-US alliance framework, how NMD can contribute to the defense of Japan, and how Japan can contribute to NMD. He also suggested what kind of defense arrangement will be desirable for promoting AMD and what kind of role Japan should play in it.[75]

Of course, while the vast American intelligence apparatus provides an information umbrella to Japan, Japanese contributions to the US are no less important. Japanese intelligence analysis capability, especially for North East Asia, is highly regarded by the US intelligence community. For example, when North Korea suffered a severe food shortage during the mid-1990s, the US Defense Intelligence Agency (DIA) estimated that North Korea would not last even a couple years. Japan's Defense Intelligence Headquarters (DIH), however, determined that North Korea could, in fact, sustain itself for years based upon Japan's own food shortage experience following World War II. Now, a decade later, the Japanese estimate was proven correct. During the Cambodian political turmoil in July 1997, both the US and Japan dispatched military units for Non-combatant Evacuation Operations (NEO). The US Armed Forces had a tremendous technical intelligence advantage from its surveillance satellites. Japan, however, had unmatched human intelligence sources in Phnom Penh. Both Armed Forces shared their intelligence and benefited each other. After the September 11 terrorist attack on the US, former Deputy Assistant Secretary of Defense (Asian & Pacific Affairs) Kurt M. Campbell mentioned on Japanese television that the Japanese financial sector must have extensive intelligence regarding financial networks of Southeast Asian terrorist organizations such as the Abu Sayyaf Group (ASG). The Japanese government has maintained friendly relations with Iran which provided much needed information about the Taliban in Afghanistan based on Iran's own armed conflict against the Taliban in September 1998. These are typical examples of intelligence interdependence. Robert Keohane and Joseph S. Nye stated in *Power and Interdependence*, 'we believe that asymmetrical interdependence can still be a source of power in a bilateral relationship.'[76]

The US Navy to Japan Maritime Self-Defense Force (JMSDF) interdependence was already established during the Cold War area. The US Navy adopted the Composite Warfare Commander (CWC) concept during the early 1980s. Normally, the highest-ranking US Naval officer was assigned as the CWC and the highest-ranking JMSDF officer was assigned as the Anti-Submarine Warfare Commander (ASWC). The ASWC reports to the CWC, but the ASWC can use not only JMSDF assets but also those of the US Navy as well. When I commanded the destroyer JDS *Yugumo*, she was assigned to conduct surveillance of the Soviet Naval exercise near the Kuril Islands. After two weeks, her fuel ran low, but no JMSDF Fast Combat Support Ship (AOE) was immediately available. AOE *Hamana* was in the dry dock, AOE *Sagami* had a fire, AOE *Towada* was dispatched to the Rim of Pacific exercise (RIMPAC), and AOE *Tokiwa* was not commissioned yet. Finally, JMSDF asked the US Seventh Fleet for assistance, and a Seventh Fleet oiler was dispatched to refuel *Yugumo*. During the Operation Enduring Freedom, JMSDF dispatched oilers for the US naval combatants in the Arabian Sea, while the US

Navy provided oilers for JMSDF combatants near the Hawaiian Islands during RIMPAC 2002. These are typical examples of the interdependent relationship between the US Navy and JMSDF. Another example was when a US Naval frigate provided intelligence regarding Soviet Naval combatants when JDS *Yugumo* could not sail beyond a certain geographic line due to political reasons.

Anne Dixon argues that the US and Japan may find a useful division of roles and missions between conflict termination (the US role) and humanitarian or economic recovery (the Japanese role) under the multinational flag of the United Nations. A concrete example of this is Operation Enduring Freedom in Afghanistan, where American troops conduct offensive operations against the Al Qaeda, and European armed forces provide an International Security Assistance Force in Kabul. This is another good example of interdependence.[77]

Those interdependence trends will clearly deepen in the future. In December 2000, Kurt Campbell argued in his paper, *Energizing the US–Japan Security Partnership*: 'Redundant investment in similar military and intelligence technologies suggest an absence of dialogue about the fundamental nature of future security cooperation. An understanding of respective roles and missions is absolutely critical to a smooth functioning and cost-effective alliance.'[78]

3. GLOBALIZATION

Laurence Martin argued in *The Global Century:*

> For various reasons, alliance or alignment seems likely to remain a pervasive feature of international politics, though one substantially modified by the new context. The unique status of the United States is a dominant feature of this changed context, and changing role of alliances will be particularly noticeable in the US case. The emergence of an embryonic 'international community,' or at least the semblance of one, will blur the margins of formal alignments, and US military forces will find themselves increasingly acting less to promote vital national interests and to achieve immediate military effects, and more to affect political behavior and mold the international system.[79]

Stephen E. Ambrose and Douglas G. Brinkley argued in *Rise to Globalism*:

> The shift emphasized the fundamentally changed nature of the American economy, from self-sufficiency to increasing dependency on others for basic supplies. America in the 1990s was richer and more powerful – and more vulnerable – than at any other time in her history.[80]

Comparing the alliances in the 20ᵗʰ century with those before that, one can find clear differences. Before the 20ᵗʰ century, alliances such as the Triple Alliance (Germany, Austria-Hungary, and Italy in 1882) were regional in nature. However, as mentioned before, the state that launches a war cannot provide the resources and industries to sustain that war without supplies from all over the world. The modern war machine requires a huge amount of munitions and energy stocks due to developed weapons. War fighters became consumers of energy and resources and therefore look to other regions for those sources. The Anglo-Japanese Alliance, formed in 1902, is the first alliance between countries several thousands of miles apart. The Rome-Berlin-Tokyo Axis of 1937 and the Atlantic Charter of 1941 were also alliances between countries several thousand of miles away from each other. NATO and America's US alliances with major Asian-Pacific countries are, of course, global in nature. For example, the Madrid Declaration on Euro-Atlantic Security and Cooperation in 1997 stated:

> We reaffirm the importance of arrangements in the Alliance for consultation on threats of a wider nature, including those linked to illegal arms trades and acts of terrorism, which affect Alliance security interest. We continue to condemn all acts of terrorism. They constitute flagrant violations of human dignity and rights and are a threat to the conduct of normal international relations. In accordance with our national legislation, we stress the need for the most effective cooperation possible to prevent and suppress this scourge.

The United Nations should address head-on ways in which to treat the above global issues. However, the present

United Nations, especially the Security Council, does not work effectively due to veto powers. Therefore, it is left to major alliances like NATO to address those contentious global issues, such as human dignity/rights and anti-terrorism. Typical examples are the 1999 Kosovo conflict and the ongoing Persian Gulf crisis. This structure becomes essentially a conflict between Western states and rogue nations. Then, the September 11 terrorist attack on the US created a combat structure between the international communities against terrorist organizations, and not the West against Islamic states. Globalization has really happened because threats and their reaction would occur anywhere in the world. For example, if Japan did not cooperate with the American attack on Iraq, Japan may not obtain American support during a North Korean crisis. This is one of the reasons why the alliances have strengthened and expanded. Admiral Thomas B. Fargo, Commander-in-Chief US Pacific Command stated: 'One of the best weapons against terrorism is the increasing cooperation between allies in the region.'[81] In other words, an alliance became a cooperative structure to solve transnational problems.

From October 1, 2002 the US created the Northern Command, which is a transnational organization to defend not only the US but also Canada and Mexico. During the continuous Persian Gulf crisis of the 1990s, Russia and China always opposed the use of force at the U.N. Security Council. Through the Kosovo conflict, NATO set a precedent by intervening without the endorsement of the United Nations when ethnic cleansing and genocide were occurring. Immediately following the September 11 terrorist attack on the US, Chinese Foreign Minister Tang Jiaxuan visited Washington, DC and said that China wanted to take action based solely upon a UN Security Council resolution. National Security Advisor Condoleezza Rice responded by saying that the US reaction is based on the self-defense right, and that a UN Security Council resolution was not required.

Today, NATO has been expanding its operational area outwards towards the east, into areas such as Afghanistan or Iraq, whereas Japan has been expanding its activities beyond its normal operational area toward the west into Iraq and the Arabian Sea. Previously, NATO issues were beyond the purview of Japan. Currently, however, the Japanese Ground Self Defense Force contingent in Iraq are strongly coordinated with the Dutch forces in Samawah and the UK and Australian military in the southeast region of Iraq; moreover, the Japanese Maritime Self-Defense ships have supplied oil to many NATO countries and non-NATO countries such as Pakistan.

Challenges of the Global Century, published by the Institute for National Strategic Studies, National Defense University in June 2001 stated:

> What is new about the structure of military globalization is that the end of the Cold War and the rash of global threats have thrown into question the rationale for an exclusively regional security system. The most important expression of regional security, NATO, has begun to expand both membership and mission, taking on a role that complements and may occasionally replace that of the UN Security Council.[82]

The Executive Summary in this document stated:

> Traditionally, security has been an external, cross-border concept. In the global era, security threats increasingly have transnational consequences. This trend had led most of the world's democracies to place a growing emphasis on new forms of security cooperation.[83]

This concern was exactly what happened on September 11, 2001. The Executive Summary also stated:

> The intelligent use of military power and maintenance of security partnerships with cooperating allies and partners are key to achieving this goal . . . Alliances and alignments will remain a pervasive feature of international politics for some time to come, even as they adapt to changing circumstances . . . This process of building coalitions can be pursued elsewhere, particularly if such efforts build on existing alliances and patterns of cooperation. In Asia, the US–Japan and US-Korea alliances are slowly being adapted to meet the needs of an emerging, more complex security environment.[84]

Regarding intelligence cooperation among the alliances, global satellite paths and ballistic missile threats from anywhere in the world make it necessary for global responsiveness. Patrick M. Cronin and Michael J. Green wrote:

> Absent a direct North Korean threat, the Japanese side will have to give more explicit support for global US deployments from Japan, based on Tokyo's shared global interests with the United States. Eventually, there will have to be further consolidation of US bases, as regional security allows and local politics demand.[85]

United States Security Strategy for Europe and NATO published in 1995 stated: 'Transatlantic cooperation is the key not only to advancing our mutual interests in Europe, but also to solving global problems.'[86] *The Alliance's Strategic Concept* approved by NATO Heads of State and Government participating in the meeting of the North Atlantic Council in Washington DC on April 23–24, 1999 stated that Alliance security must also take into account the global context. Alliance security interests can be affected by other risks of a wider nature, including acts of terrorism, sabotage and organized crime, and by the disruption of flow of vital resources. The uncontrolled movement of large numbers of people, particularly as a consequence of armed conflicts, can also pose problems for security and stability affecting the Alliance.[87] The Sydney Statement, the Joint Security Declaration between Australia and the US of 1996, stated that their common agenda seeks a secure and prosperous future for both countries, the Asia Pacific region and the global community.

The Common Agenda for Cooperation in Global Perspective, launched in July of 1993, is an important example of how Japan and the US work together on critical global issues to improve the future of the world. The agenda comprises:

- Promoting Health and Human Development: Women in Development (WID), Global Food Supply, Population and Health (Incl. Children's health & HIV/AIDS), and Emerging and Reemerging Infections Diseases
- Responding to Challenges to Global Stability: Counternarcotics, Civil Society and Democratization, Counterterrorism, and National and Man-made Disaster Reduction

- Protecting the Global Environment: Conservation (Incl. Policy dialogue, coral reefs, forests), Development Assistance for the Environment, Global Observation Information Network, Regional Network/ Institutes for Global Change Research, Environmental and Energy-efficient Technologies, and Environmental Education
- Advancing Science and Technology: Civil Industrial Technology, Transportation, and Educational Technology for the 21st Century.

Since its inception, the common Agenda has already been successful in various areas, such as:

- Through vaccination programs, polio has virtually been eradicated in the Western Pacific area and steps continue to be taken to eliminate the disease.
- In Peru, a crop substitution program has commercialized the indigenous 'camu-camu' plant, thus reducing the farmers' economic dependence on crops used in the production of narcotics.
- Japan has provided extensive assistance to US non-profit organizations such as the Nature Conservancy to help in such fields as the conservation of bio-diversity in Central and South America.

Former US Labor Secretary Robert B. Reich wrote in *The Work of Nations*:

> It is not simply a matter of national security. Modern technologies have diffused global power. Even relatively poor nations can now finance weapons of fierce destruction. It is, rather, a matter of national purpose. Are we still a society, even if we are no longer an economy? Are we bound together by something more than the gross national product? Or has the idea of the nation-state as a collection of people sharing some responsibility for their mutual well-being become passé?[88]

At the 21st Systems and Technology Forum in Tokyo in January 2000, then Under Secretary of Defense for Acquisition and Technology, Dr Jacques S. Gansler, mentioned in his opening remarks:

The industrial environment of the Twenty First Century also presents challenges. Industry – even defense industry – is becoming multinational and transnational . . . We will have to find ways to accommodate industrial competition and collaboration across international borders.

He elaborated on this idea at the agenda of *Observation on Globalization* by saying that a Team A which consists of both Japanese and US companies will compete against a Team B, which consists of other Japanese and US companies. He added that threats are becoming so global in nature that alliances must work together to cope with them. He also gave two concrete examples: first; when both Japanese and US AEGIS destroyers patrol at sea against rogue nations' ballistic missile threats, the targets which the US radar detect would be destroyed by the Japanese missile. Second, US forces may use Japanese spare parts in Japanese depots and vice versa. The Japan-US Joint Declaration on Security-Alliance for the 21st Century stated that the Prime Minister and the President recognized that the Treaty of Mutual Cooperation and Security is the core of the Japan-US Alliance, and underlines the mutual confidence that constitutes the foundation for bilateral cooperation on global issues.[89]

In November 1996, a refugee crisis was building in east Zaire, and the Japanese Government studied the possibility of conducting peacekeeping operations there. As the Japanese Defense Attaché in Washington DC, I heard a briefing about this situation from the Pentagon. Lieutenant Colonel Robin Sakoda, then Japan desk officer in the Office of the Secretary of Defense, also attended the briefing. I said to him: 'You are very busy not only for the US–Japan alliance but also Africa.' Lieutenant Colonel Sakoda immediately responded: 'No, this is the US–Japan alliance.' In reality, information exchange between the US and Japan is an important element of the alliance no matter where a crisis exists. The Japanese side also provided a briefing to Pentagon officials regarding the lessons learned from the Tokyo subway sarin gas attack incident. Transnational terrorism should be responded to with international effort.

In November 1998, Japan Self-Defense Forces were dispatched for international emergency rescue operations to Honduras, which had suffered tremendous damage due to Hurricane Mitch. At that time, US armed forces provided much-needed support, including logistics from Kelly Air Force Base in Texas and ground transportation in Honduras. In November 1999, the Japan Air Self-Defense Force (JASDF) dispatched several C-130s for the international peace cooperation effort to help East Timorese displaced persons, and American intelligence was very helpful for the Japanese troops involved. American intelligence again helped the JASDF's humanitarian rescue operation (HRO) in Pakistan, which provided tents for the refugees. Shortly afterwards the US commenced Operation Enduring Freedom (OEF) in September 2001. About 700 Japan Ground Self-Defense Force (JGSDF) personnel were dispatched to East Timor in the spring of 2002 and US intelligence again provided assistance with situational awareness.

US armed forces have rescued many Japanese citizens in failed states such as Albania (1997), Eritrea (1998) and Sierra Leone (1998). Japan cannot conduct those types of operations by herself. Even if Japan cannot participate in military operations abroad, the US–Japan alliance does work in not only Asia, but also Africa, Central America, Europe and the rest of the world. Such cooperation would have been inconceivable at the beginning of the last century. The US also depends on the Japanese for forward deployment bases in the global context. The American forward bases in Japan provide not only for North East Asian security, but they also contribute to the stabilization of other regions including the Middle East. The early stages of the 1991 Persian Gulf crisis offered a powerful example of such strategic benefits: Marines from Okinawa (as well as elsewhere) were quickly in place to deter Iraq from attacking Saudi Arabia.[90] In July 1997, the US Pacific Command formulated Joint Task Force (JTF) 510 for the Cambodian crisis. The US aircraft carrier USS *Independence* and her battle group that had been forward stationed in Yokosuka got underway for the Persian Gulf crisis of January 1998. In that same month, the 31ˢᵗ Marine Expeditionary Unit (MEU) in Okinawa was dispatched for the situation in Indonesia. In November 1998, USS *Belleau*

Wood and two other amphibious ships that were stationed in Sasebo deployed to the Gulf. 31st MEU was on alert when a North Korean semi-submerged vessel intruded into South Korean territorial waters in December 1998. The USS *Theodore Roosevelt* carrier battle group, which was supposed to deploy for the Gulf from Norfolk, instead participated in Operation Allied Force in Kosovo in April 1999. The USS *Kitty Hawk* carrier battle group, home ported in Yokosuka, was dispatched to the Gulf instead. 31st MEU was again dispatched to East Timor in September 1999. The USS *Kitty Hawk* got underway for the Arabian Sea after the September 11 terrorist attack in 2001. Again, the USS *Kitty Hawk* carrier battle group was dispatched to the Persian Gulf during the Iraqi crisis in February 2003. Following the massive Tsunami in South Asia in December 2004, JTF 536 headed by Marine Corps General Blackman stationed in Okinawa was formulated and deployed to Utapao, Thailand. These were not easy tasks for the US Navy and Marines in any situation, but they were made easier because these forces were forward based in Japan. The five guiding precepts for the American Global Defense Posture announced on November 25, 2003 were: first, create flexibility to contend with uncertainty; second, strengthen allied roles; third, work within and across regions; fourth, promote an expeditionary approach, and fifth, focus on capabilities, not numbers.[91] Taking a cue from the past activities of US forces stationed in Japan as mentioned above, their role will be much more important and the US–Japan alliance must be strengthened in the future. Japanese Prime Minister Koizumi stated at the 50th anniversary of the signing of the San Francisco Peace Treaty in September 2001: 'The role that Japan and the United States should take is large, and the significance of the Japan-US alliance is becoming bigger and bigger, not only for both countries, but for the Asia-pacific region and the entire world.'

There are two global rationales for strengthening the US–Japan alliance – active and passive roles. The active role describes how Japan and the US work together on critical global issues to improve the future of the world. Only post-modern sphere countries can do these active roles. The passive role describes how Japan and the US defend each other against transnational threats and what must be done in conjunction with modern sphere countries like China and Russia.

Regarding the passive role, the world has been shrinking and the nature of threats has been changing due to the development of rapid transportation and electronic communications. The threat used to be from a state itself. Recently, however, we have to pay attention to non-state threats,[92] such as criminal destabilization, international terrorism, proliferation of weapons of mass destruction, drug trade, piracy, illegal immigration, refugee problems, environment abuse, and information warfare. Threats have become more transnational and global, and therefore, each advanced country must cooperate to engage them successfully.

Former Secretary of Defense William S. Cohen spoke to the Council on Foreign Relations in September 1998. His speech, entitled 'Security in a Grave New World', identified three categories of threats: (1) transnational terrorism; (2) the spread of weapons of mass destruction; (3) ethnic, religious, economic tensions that undermine the security and stability of the world. Then he mentioned that the US national security policy basically rests upon four essential pillars: (1) bipartisan support for security policy; (2) budgets that are adequate to support our objectives; (3) international cooperation; (4) interagency cooperation.

In *The National Security Strategy For A New Century*, published by the White House in December 1999, *Threats to US Interests* include: regional or state-centered threats; transnational threats; spread of dangerous technologies; failed states; foreign intelligence collection; environmental and health threats. Regarding transnational threats, this document stated:

> There are threats that do not respect national borders and which often arise from non-states actors, such as terrorists and criminal organizations. They threaten US interests, values and citizens – in the United States and abroad. Examples include terrorism, drug trafficking and other international crime, illicit arms trafficking, uncontrolled refugee migration, and trafficking in human beings, particularly women and children. We also face threats to national infrastructures, which increasingly could take the form of cyber-attacks in addition to physical attacks or

sabotage, and could originate from terrorist or criminal groups as well as hostile states.[93]

On May 6, 1997, the Declaration of the Mexican/US Alliance against drugs was formulated. The declaration stated: 'Drug abuse and drug trafficking are a danger to our societies, an affront to our sovereignty, and a threat to our national security. We declare our nations united in alliance to combat this menace.'[94] This declaration shows us that alliances are formed not only to counter state threats, but non-state threats as well. On May 7, 2002, the Government of the Indonesia, Malaysia, and the Republic of the Philippines made the Agreement on Information Exchange and Establishment of Communication Procedures in order to counter transnational crimes and terrorism.[95]

Former Chairman of Japan's Joint Staff Council, Admiral Kazuya Natsukawa, made an office call to former US Deputy Secretary of Defense, Dr John Hamre, in March 1998. The first question initiated by Dr Hamre was how Japan's Self-Defense Forces would defend against cyber terrorism. Almost two years later, many Japanese ministries and agencies were severely attacked by computer hackers. Administrative Vice Minister of Defense, Ken Sato, dispatched several cyber hacker specialists to the US Department of Defense in the winter of 2000. These information exchanges, based on the US–Japan alliance, are typical examples of how the alliance works to counter global threats.

In December 1996, the Peruvian terrorist group Tupac Amaru occupied the Japanese Ambassador's official residence in Lima, Peru, and took hostages for four months. Right after the incident, I, as the Japanese Defense Attaché in Washington DC, went to the Defense Intelligence Agency (DIA) in the Pentagon and tried to gather information regarding the incident. I found out that the DIA had two indications in the past month that Tupac Amaru would attack a certain public organization. Therefore, if the Japanese Embassy in Lima had had a defense attaché, as well as a close information exchange relationship with the US Defense Attaché there, this incident might have been avoided and the Japanese Government would have saved a tremendous amount of time, money, labor, and mental pressure. This is another example of how alliance coordination can be effective against transnational threats. *The United States and Japan: Advancing Toward a Mature Partnership*, Institute for National Strategic Studies Special Report in October 2000 emphasized that transnational issues, such as illegal immigration, international crime, and terrorism all require coordinated interagency programs in both countries.[96]

Defeating Terrorism – New Strategy for the Campaign Against Terrorism, published by the Center for Strategic & International Studies (CSIS) on November 27, 2001 stated:

> Will the United States be able to promote a consensus on definitions of 'terrorism' and 'terrorism of global reach' as it seeks to assemble the broadest possible coalition to wage this campaign . . . Vice President Richard Cheney predicted that the coming conflict would be 'global in scope.' What is also true but less understood is that this will be the first major conflict to occur in the age of globalization.[97]

To Prevail – An American Strategy for the Campaign against Terrorism, also published by CSIS, stated:

> Success will require a fundamentally new approach on the part of the United States and its coalition partners around the world. One of best ways to fight a network is to create a network of our own. The United States and its international partners must build their own global network of intelligence, law enforcement, military, financial, diplomatic, and other instruments to successfully take on global terrorist organizations like Al Qaeda . . . The aftermath of the crisis has validated those who favor a strong focus on alliance relationships in the formulation and execution of US foreign policy. Long-standing security ties, such as the NATO alliance and our bilateral alliances with countries like Japan, are serving as the building blocks for the various anti terror coalitions.[98]

In all probability, alliances among the post-modern sphere nations as described by Robert Cooper will evolve into a multinational, advanced 'country club', like G-7 summits, designed to cope with global threats, such as rogue countries and non-state actors mentioned above. In other words, wealthy nations, which can obtain the most benefit under the current world system, want to maintain the *status quo* of stability. Recent incidents underscore this observation. *National Security Strategy of the United States*, published in 1991, defined a 'new world order' as 'global community based on our democratic values', which is possible by development of global information and communications.[99] After the Cold War, the US and other post-modern-sphere countries joined together in coalition warfare against Iraq, the Federal Republic of Yugoslavia and Afghanistan (Taliban). Slobodan Milosevich and Saddam Husein finally buckled under relentless pressure. The Korean crisis in 1993–4 provided another example for a rogue country. The idea of Trilateralism – cooperation among the industrialized democracies of Western Europe, Japan, and North America – has been initiated since there exist many issues of common interest to these countries, including sharing of democratic values, market economies, and globalism.[100] In the Pacific region, the idea of some kind of alliance among the US, Japan, ROK, and Australia has also been discussed.[101] In 2002, Japan shared terrorism information with the ROK for the 2002 FIFA World Cup soccer competition, which took place in Japan and Korea. Japan Self-Defense Forces exchanged intelligence with Australia regarding East Timor's security.

Piracy on the high seas, for example, is now a major transnational concern. Piracy incidents have been increasing dramatically in the past ten years.[102] Reported attacks against commercial ships have tripled over the past decade, increasing in 1999 alone by 40 percent.[103] Nearly two-thirds of the attacks in 1999 occurred in Asia, with 113 of the 285 reported cases taking place in Indonesia's waters and ports. The risk of attacks is increasing with 90 percent of the world's trade moving via ship and 45 percent of all shipping moving through the pirate-infested waters of Asia. Clearly, piracy is becoming an increasing threat to global trade.[104] Based upon the Alondra Rainbow's piracy incident in the Strait of Malacca in October 1999, then Prime Minister Obuchi of Japan proposed a counter-piracy conference at the ASEAN summit in November 1999. A conference was held in April 2000 in Tokyo, and participation included not only ASEAN countries like Indonesia, Malaysia, and Singapore, but also ROK and China. Indian Minister of Defense, George Fernandes visited Japan in January 2000 and proposed to then Director, Japan Defense Agency, Kawara, a combined anti-piracy exercise. Eventually, an Indian Coast Guard vessel recovered the Alondra Rainbow. This is a typical example of global coalition against a non-state actor threat. In this case, it became quite difficult to define the vessel's nationality. Since there are so many *Flags of Convenience* ships, the idea of *Flag State Control* became *Port State Control.*

The most important task for an alliance relationship has become sharing the international norm for stability. Up through the 19ᵗʰ century, war was essentially a local phenomenon. However, war became a global operation in the 20ᵗʰ century and this trend will become more intensive in the 21ˢᵗ century. We can no longer think of national security as a local matter without a global dimension. In other words, a nation cannot fight by herself. Alliances are now fundamental to any war-fighting operation. Robert Keohane and Joseph S. Nye argued in *Power and Interdependence,*

> Militarily, the US alliance with Japan became an integral part of US global military planning, and the military interdependence helped to mitigate the frictions (maintaining stability) that arose in the trade relations between the two countries in the 1990s. More broadly, Japan became part of the US-centered security community, so global relations of complex interdependence came to characterize its relationships with the United States and Western Europe.[105]

In any case, Western alliances created in the Cold War era will not disband in the foreseeable future. However, each state has its own national interests and different threat perceptions. Recent events give the impression that military operations are conducted by *ad hoc* 'coalition of willingness' rather than the formal alliances. There are two-coalition groups in the US Central Command, Tampa Florida – Operation Enduring Freedom (OEF) against Al Qaeda, Taliban and Operation Iraqi Freedom (OIF). Another example of a formal coalition would be the Proliferation Security Initiative and Ballistic Missile Defense network. While, if a conflict

were to happen on the Korean Peninsula, a coalition of willingness would be formed among America, Japan, ROK,
Australia, probably Canada and maybe others to deal with
that conflict. Many Western countries, which have similar
national interests, get together for a common and specific
purpose.

In examining why alliances expand and strengthen even
after the threats have diminished, much analysis has focused
on European alliances, including *Constructivism* as mentioned before. There are few analyses focusing on the Pacific
alliances, which consist of American alliances with Japan,
ROK, and Australia. Among these three alliances, the US-ROK
alliance is not an appropriate example. The ROK has been
facing a real threat from North Korea, during and after the
Cold War. As well, the US-Australia alliance is also not a
good example. Australia did not face an imminent threat
even during the Cold War era. Therefore, we will examine the
rationale utilizing the US–Japan alliance as a suitable
example. The Japan-US Joint Declaration on Security-
Alliance For The 21st Century – inaugurated in April 1996 –
sought as an alliance rationale not outside common threats
but common internal values such as freedom, democracy,
market economy and human rights.[106] However, it has been
difficult to explain alliance rationales in general and
America's shift in particular by using value sharing according
to international developments. The US attitude to seek its
national interests has been more realistic, effective and dominant. Therefore, we have to redefine the US–Japan alliance
rationale again.

By looking at a number of case studies I believe the
above theory can be proved. At the same time, I will examine
not only rational factors, which serve to strengthen the
US–Japan alliance, but also those that weaken it. When
doing that, I will review the Japanese alliance history in
Chapter 2, examine the alliance rationale for Japan in
Chapter 3, for the US in Chapter 4, for the other Asian countries in Chapter 5, then explore current issues in Chapter 6,
predict future case studies in Chapter 7, and finally provide
negative factors for the alliance in Chapter 8.

NOTES

1   Charles W. Freeman, Jr., *The Diplomat's Dictionary*, Third printing, Washington, DC: United States Institute of Peace Press, 2001, p. 11

2   Hans J. Morgenthau Revised by Kenneth W. Thompson, *Politics Among Nations Brief Edition*, McGraw-Hill, Inc., 1993, p. 197

3   Kenneth N. Waltz, *Theory of International Politics* Fifth Edition, McGraw-Hill, Inc., 1979, p. 126

4   Kenneth N. Waltz, 'The Emerging Structure of International Politics', *International Security*, Vol. 18, No. 2, Fall 1993, pp. 66–67

5   Stephen M. Walt, *The Origins of Alliance*, Cornell University Press, 1987, p. 17

6   K. J. Holsti, *International Politics* Sixth Edition, University of British Columbia, 1992, p. 89

7   John J. Mearsheimer, 'Back to the Future: Instability in Europe After the Cold War', *International Security*, Vol. 15 No. 1, Summer 1990

8   Charles W. Kegley, Jr., and Gregory A. Raymond, *When Trust Breaks Down: Alliance Norms and World Politics*, University of South Carolina Press, 1990, p. 208

9   NATO's Strategic Concept, by the Heads of State and Governments Part II-Strategic Perspectives, The Evolving Strategic Environment, Paragraph 12, 1999

10 Remarks of Deputy Secretary Wolfowitz, *Speech at the 38ᵗʰ Munich Conference on Security Policy*, February 2, 2002

11 *NATO-Russia Relations: A New Quality, Declaration by Heads of States and Government of NATO Member States and the Russian Federation*, May 28, 2002

12 *United States Security Strategy for the East Asia-Pacific Region*, DOD-ISA Feb. 1995

13 *The United States Security Strategy for the East Asia-Pacific Region (EASR)*, Secretary of Defense, Nov. 1998

14 *A National Security Strategy for a New Century*, The White House, December 1999, p. 34

15 *The United States and Asia: Toward a New US Strategy and Force Posture*, Rand, May 2001, summary xvi, xvii

16 *The National Security Strategy of the United States of America*, The White House, September 2002, p. 5

[17] *National Defense Program Guideline for FY 2005 and After*, Government of Japan, December 2004, p. 6

[18] *US Department of State, International Information Programs*, Washington File, 18 February 2002

[19] Charles W. Kegley, Jr., and Gregory A. Raymond, *When Trust Breaks Down: Alliance Norms and World Politics*, University of South Carolina Press, 1990, p. 209

[20] *Quadrennial Defense Review Report*, US Department of Defense, September 30, 2001, pp. 14, 15

[21] *28th ROK-US Security Consultative Meeting Joint Communiqué* November 1, 1996, Washington, DC

[22] Ralph A. Cossa, *US-Korea-Japan Relations: Building Toward a 'Virtual Alliance'*, the Pacific Forum CSIS, December 3 1999

[23] *Australia-United States: A Strategic partnership for the twenty-first Century*, Jul. 1996

[24] Yoichi Funabashi, *Domei no Hikaku Kenkyu*, Nihon Hyoron Sha, 2001 pp. 95–96

[25] President Clinton, 'Address to a Joint Sitting of the House of Parliament' *Current House Hansard*, 20 November 1996, pp. 4–5

[26] Australia-US Ministerial Consultation, *Joint Communiqué*, 1997

[27] *The United States Security Strategy for the East Asia-Pacific Region*, US Department of Defense, November 23 1998, p. 26

[28] Ibid.

[29] *Testimony at Budget Hearing before the Senate Foreign Relations Committee*, US Department of States, February 5, 2002

[30] ESAR, 1998, p. 12

[31] *Defense News*, March 8, 1999

[32] Andrew F. Krepinevich, *Transforming America's Alliances*, Center for Strategic and Budgetary Assessments, February 2000, pp. 11, 13

[33] Yoichi Funabashi, *Domei no Hikaku Kenkyu*, Nihon Hyoron Sha, March 2001, p. 177

[34] Charles W. Kegley Jr., Gregory A. Raymond, *When Trust Breaks Down*, University of south Carolina Press, 1990, p. 59

[35] The *United States Security Strategy for the East Asia-Pacific Region 1998* stated: 'The United States welcomes the public statements of ROK President Kim Dae-Jung affirming the value of bilateral alliance and US military presence even after reunification of the Korean peninsula. The US strongly agrees that

our alliance and military presence will continue to support stability both on the Korean Peninsula and throughout the region after North Korea is no longer a threat.'

36 Thomas Risse-Kappen, *Collective Identity in a Democratic Community: The Case of NATO in The Culture of National Security*, Columbia University Press, 1996, p. 357

37 Thomas Risse-Kappen, *Cooperation Among democracies: The European Influence On US Foreign Policy*, Princeton University Press, 1995, p. 219

38 Thomas Risse-Kappen, *Collective Identity in a Democratic Community: The Case of NATO in The Culture of National Security*, Columbia University Press, 1996, p. 397

39 Thomas Risse-Kappen, *Cooperation Among democracies: The European Influence On US Foreign Policy*, Princeton University Press, 1995, p. 195

40 Captain Moreland, Ota, Pan'kov, *Naval Cooperation in the Pacific: Looking to the Future*, Center for International Security and Arms Control in Stanford University, February 1993

41 *Agreement between the Government of Australia and the Government of the Republic Indonesia on maintaining security*, Jakarta, 18 December 1995

42 *China's National Defense in 2000*, The information office of the state council the People's Republic of China, October 2000, pp. 5–6

43 *China's National Defense in 2004*, The information office of the state council the People's Republic of China, December 2004, p. 4

44 Japan-US Joint Declaration on Security-Alliance for the 21st Century, 17 April 1996, No. 4

45 *National Defense Program Guideline for FY 2005 and After*, Government of Japan, December 2004, p. 6

46 Michael J. Green and Patrick M. Cronin, *The US–Japan Alliance: Past, Present, and Future*, 1999, introduction xiii

47 Michael Mandelbaum, 'The Bush Foreign Policy', *Foreign Affairs*, Vol. 70, No. 1, 1991, p. 13

48 *United States Security Strategy for the East Asia-Pacific Region 1998*, US Department of Defense, Office of International Security Affairs, P. 62

49 Banning Garret and Nonnie Glaser, 'China's Pragmatic Posture toward the Korean Peninsula', *Korean Journal of Defense Analysis*, vol. 9, no. 2, Winter 1997, p. 87

[50] Narushige Michishita, 'Alliance After Peace in Korea', *Survival*, Autumn 1999, The IISS Quarterly, pp. 72–73

[51] Michael Mandelbaum, *The Bush Foreign Policy*, Foreign Affairs, circa 1991–2

[52] *London Declaration on a transformed North Atlantic Alliance* issued by the Heads of States and Government of the North Atlantic Council, London, July 5–6, 1990

[53] *United States Security Strategy for Europe and NATO*, US Department of Defense, Washington, DC, 1995

[54] Madrid Declaration on Euro-Atlantic Security and Cooperation 8th July 1997 Item 4, p. 2

[55] Funabashi Yoichi, *Doumei no Hikaku Kenkyu*, Nihon Hyouronn Sha, March 2001, p. 182

[56] *The Alliance's Strategic Concept*, approved by the Heads of State and Government participating in the meeting of North Atlantic Council in Washington DC on 23rd and 24th April 1999, paragraph 13

[57] Statement on combating terrorism: Adapting the Alliance's Defense Capabilities, NATO Press Releases No. 2, 18 December 2001

[58] Narushige Michishita, 'Alliances After Peace in Korea', *Survival* (The International Institute for Strategic Studies Quarterly) Autumn 1999, p. 72

[59] Richard J. Samuels and Christopher P. Twomey, *Eagle Eyes the Pacific: American Foreign Policy Options in East Asia after the Cold War*, The Council on Foreign Relations, 1999, pp. 6–7

[60] Selig Harrison, *Japan's Nuclear Future: The Plutonium Debate and East Asian Security*, Carnegie Endowment for International Peace, 1996, p. 26

[61] *Quadrennial Defense Review Report*, Department of Defense, September 30, 2001, pp. 14, 15

[62] 'A New National Partnership' speech by Secretary of State Henry A. Kisshinger at Los Angeles, January 24, 1975 News Release, Department of States, Bureau of Public Affairs, Office of Media Service, p. 1

[63] Thomas Risse-Kappen, *Cooperation Among Democracies*, Princeton University Press, 1995, p. 217

[64] *Prospects for Global Order*, Royal Institute of International Affairs, London 1993 pp. 8–24

[65] Treaty of Mutual Cooperation and Security Between Japan and US, June 23, 1960 Treaty

66 Tyson Laura D'Andrea, *Who's Bashing Whom?*, Institute for International Economics, 1992

67 Robert O. Keohane and Joseph S. Nye, *Power and Interdependence*, Longman, 2001, pp. 100, 130

68 Gregg A. Rubinstein, *US–Japan Armaments Cooperation*, The Council on Foreign Relations, 1999, p. 280

69 Robert Keohane and Joseph S. Nye, *Power and Interdependence*, Boston, 1989, pp. 3–4

70 Norman Angell, *Great Illusion*, Garland Pub, 1912

71 *The Joint Staff Officer's Guide 2000, JFSC Pub 1*, pp. 1–19

72 David S. Alberts, John J. Garstka, Frederic P. Stein, *Network Centric Warfare-Developing and Leveraging Information Superiority-*, Department of Defense, August 1999, p. 226

73 *The Alliance's Strategic Concept* approved by NATO Heads of State and Government participating in the meeting of North Atlantic Council in Washington DC in April 1999, Guideline for Alliance's Force Posture, paragraph 52

74 *Quadrennial Defense Review Report*, Department of Defense, September 30 2001, p. 9

75 Futoshi Shibayama, *Japan-US Defense Cooperation and the Road to Alliance Missile Defense (AMD)*, The journal of International Security, Vol. 29, No. 4, March 2002

76 Robert Keohane and Joseph S. Nye, *Power and Interdependence*, Boston 1989, p. 252

77 Michael J. Green and Patrick M. Cronin, *The US–Japan Alliance: Past, Present, and Future*,1999, introduction, p. xvii

78 Kurt M. Campbell, *Energizing the US–Japan Security Partnership*, The Washington Quarterly Autumn 2000, p. 131

79 Laurence Martin, *The Global Century, Chapter 27 Alliances and Alignments in a Globalization World*, Institute for National Strategic Studies, National Defense University, 2001, p. 599

80 Stephen E. Ambrose and Douglas G. Brinkley, *Rise to Globalism*, Penguin Books, 1997, p. xiv

81 Admiral Fargo's speech at the biennial conference of the Asia-Pacific Center for Security Studies, July 2002

82 *Challenges of the Global Century*, Institute for National Strategic Studies National Defense University, June 2001, p. 56

83 *Challenges of the Global Century (Executive Summary)*, Institute for National Strategic Studies National Defense University, June 2001, p. 18

84 Ibid, p. 21
85 Patrick M. Cronin and Michael J. Green, *From Reaffirmation to Redefinition–An Agenda for the Future*, The Council on Foreign Relations, 1999, p. 320
86 *United States Security Strategy for Europe and NATO*, US Department of Defense, Washington, DC, 1995
87 *The Alliance's Strategic Concept* by NATO Heads of State and Government participating in the meeting of the North Atlantic Council in Washington DC on April 23–24, 1999, Paragraph 24
88 Robert B. Reich, *The Work of Nations*, Vintage Books, 1992, p. 9
89 Japan-US Joint Declaration on Security-Alliance for the 21st century – 8th item
90 Paul S. Giarra, *US Bases in Japan: Historical Background and Innovative Approaches*, The Council on Foreign Relations, 1999, p. 130
91 *Defense Department Background Briefing on Global Defense Posture*, United States Department of Defense, November 25, 2003
92 *1999 Strategic Assessment* Institute for National Strategic Studies, National Defense University, pp. 245–260
93 *A National Security Strategy For A New Century*, The White House, December 1999, pp. 2–3
94 *Declaration of the Mexican/US alliance against drugs*, Mexico City, May 6, 1997
95 *Agreement on Information Exchange and Establishment of Communication Procedures*, Putrajaya Malaysia, May 7 2002
96 *The United States and Japan: Advancing Toward a Mature Partnership*, Institute for National Strategic Studies National Defense Studies, October 2000, p. 5
97 *Defeating Terrorism – New Strategy for the Campaign Against Terrorism*, Center for Strategic & International Studies (CSIS) on November 27, 2001, pp. 4 and 6
98 *To Prevail – An American Strategy for the Campaign against Terrorism*, CSIS, November 2001, pp. 302, 305, and 306
99 *National Security Strategy of the United States*, Washington, DC, August 1991
100 *Managing the International System over the Next Ten Years: A Report to the trilateral Commission*, The Trilateral Commission New York, Paris and Tokyo, July 1997, p. 39

[101] Robert B. Zoellick, *A Republican Foreign Policy, Foreign Affairs,* January/February 2000 pp. 74–75

[102] Lieutenant Commander I.D.H. Wood, Canadian Navy, *Piracy Is Deadlier Than Ever,* US Naval Institute Proceedings, January 2000, pp. 60–63

[103] *Piracy and Armed Robbery Against Ships* Annual Report 1 January–31 December 1999, International Chamber of Commerce, International Maritime Bureau, January 2000, p. 10

[104] Dana R. Dillon, *Piracy in Asia: A Growing Barrier to Maritime Trade,* Heritage Foundation, June 22 2000

[105] Robert Keohane and Joseph S. Nye, *Power and Interdependence,* Longman, 2001, p. 240

[106] Japan-US Joint Declaration on Security-Alliance for the 21st century – 2nd item

2

Historical Review

Excluding the Japan-Korean Alliance from February 1904 to the Korean annexation by Japan August 1910, Japan has had three alliances in the modern age. Japan's first ally was the United Kingdom, from 1902 to 1921. The second alliance was with Hitler's Germany and Mussolini's Italy, the so-called Rome-Berlin-Tokyo axis, from 1936 to 1945. The third alliance is with the United States, established in 1952 and continues through today. Through historical review, we find that trust is the key to maintaining an alliance. Charles W. Kegley, Jr., and Gregory A. Raymond stated in their book *When Trust Breaks Down* that in an international crisis prevailing alliance norms may influence decisions to honor commitments and thereby determine whether alliances make the expected contribution to mutual security.[1]

1. LESSONS LEARNED FROM ANGLO-JAPANESE ALLIANCE

Japan's biggest mistake in modern diplomatic history was breaking off the Anglo-Japanese alliance after World War I. The US–Japan alliance relations today are similar to the Anglo-Japanese alliance that ended after World War I.

Both Anglo-Japanese alliances' primary threat came from the North – Russia and the Soviet Union. During the initial alliances, the power balance was Tri-Polar, the US-Europe-Japan. In both alliances, Japan allied with the naval super-power of the day, the UK in 1902 and the US in 1952. The results of major wars during those alliance periods, the

Russo-Japanese War and the Cold War, were successful for our side. However, Japanese military contributions to World War I and the Gulf War were not considered adequate by much of the world as would be expected from a full alliance partner. Japan only sent its Naval Escort Squadron to the Mediterranean towards the end of World War I and the only military contribution to the first Persian Gulf War was the deployment of Japan Maritime Self-Defense Force Mine Sweeping Squadron to the Persian Gulf. After the Cold War, many people in Japan have expressed support for creating a multinational security arrangement in East Asia[2] similar to the situation in the 1920s.

The United Kingdom begun to trust Japan following the Boxer Rebellion in 1899. British solders were deeply impressed by the Japanese soldier's bravery and ethical behavior. This was the origin of Anglo-Japanese Alliance of 1902. However, after the Russo-Japanese War and World War I, the United Kingdom begun to distrust Japan. The British Naval Attaché in Japan, Captain E.H. Rymer, RN, made a report to the Admiralty in 1918 entitled 'Japan at War from 1914.'[3] He stated:

Japan's aim in this war is: -
(1) To make of it the greatest commercial success possible.
(2) To give what aid it does in the most unostentatious manner, (presumably to avoid hurting the susceptibilities of the Germans).
It must be understood that all her actions are governed by these two considerations.

German Sentiment in Japan.

Practically all the members of professional and medical professions are German trained, while the Army is modeled exclusively on that of Germany. There is therefore a very large section of the population who, if they cannot be described as pro-German, must certainly be said to have very pronounced German leanings.

Incidentally, it may be remarked that any friendly feeling they possess for Germany rests purely on a selfish basis. A German is, to a Japanese, just as much a foreigner as is an Englishman or a Frenchman, and in adopting German manners and customs the Japanese do so because they think that they are getting the best value for their money.

It would be a mistake, for instance, to put down Japan's very humane treatment of German prisoners to any false motives of friendship or humanity, it is only done to give a reputation for such, and to be on the safe side in case. Anyone having any doubt on this subject is recommended to study the so-called colonizing methods of the Japanese in Korea, and Formosa, which are distinguished by about as much humanity as the Germans showed the Hereros.

Naval and Military Assistance to the Allied Cause.

Naval. Japan, provided it does not clash with the principles referred to in the opening paragraph, is prepared to give a considerable amount of indirect, and a certain amount of direct naval assistance. It is noticeable, however, that the Minister of Marine invariably defends the latter by stating that it is afforded chiefly to protect Japanese shipping interests, through certainly, so far as the T.B.D.'s in the Mediterranean are concerned, this is quite untrue.

The inability to use the same excuse to cover the sale or loan of Battle Cruisers is probably why they refuse to consider this suggestion.

Military. It is useless to expect them to send an army to Europe. It would be in direct opposition to these two guiding principles, while it would be most unpopular with the Japanese people, the vast majority of whom, have always looked upon the war as one between European nations, with useful local pickings, to be had for the asking by Japan.

It is extremely doubtful too whether the Army Chiefs would care to risk their reputation against, and among the trained armies of Europe. They should know, if they do not, that their Army is at least 5 years behind, and that the intelligence and initiative of their soldiers and officers is of a very low order as compared with a European standard.

Added to this they have neither an Air nor a Motor Transport Service, nor are they likely to have in the near future. The best technical observers are of options that they will never make good fliers, while a very few months acquaintance with the Japanese chauffeur is sufficient to demonstrate his inability to 'run' a petrol engine.

They might send troops to Eastern Siberia, but if they did it would only be because such action was necessary to protect their own interests.

In considering the question of military assistance it must be remembered that the idea of the defeat of the German Army by the British is always unpalatable to the Chiefs of the Japanese Army. They have adopted the Prussian system *in toto*, and if that system breaks down there will always be the feeling that they have 'backed the wrong horse'.

Shipping. As it is distinctly opposed to their two guiding principles, it can easily be understood why the Japanese have always refused to allocate any considerable portion of their shipping to supply the Allied deficiency in this respect. The Japanese Government too depend so much on magnates, to risk cutting into their profits.

Political. The present Japanese Government is probably as good a one, from the Allies' point of view, as could be got together. Most of its members realize and admit that Japan owes her independence, her prosperity and her existence to the Alliance, and that the Alliance must be considered for years as the keystone of their policy (provided the Allies come out of this war successfully).

But it would be the greatest mistake to imagine that any Japanese is anything at heart but absolutely pro-Japanese and anti-foreign. Many of them, particularly Naval officers, politicians, and business men who have travelled and been trained in Europe, have a great personal liking for European nations, however, the Japanese do not know the meaning of gratitude, nor have they any intention of making any considerable self sacrifice for any other nation. Consider for example the miserable fiasco known as the 'Mission of Sympathy', the object of which was to collect a large sum of money for the Allies. After a most degrading exhibition of 'touting', some £200,000 was raised, of which at least a third was contributed by the Imperial Household, Mitsui, Mitsubishi, and one or two other firms, while at the same time shipping 'narikins' were spending their quickly gained wealth on Geisha dinners at £10 a head, and other less respectable orgies.

Our own inability to understand them and our practice of dealing with them as a Western instead of an Oriental nation, has a great deal to do with the fact that they have not shown more enthusiasm for the war.

We have never sufficiently impressed them, and though they realize our strength, because we have never shown it, they think themselves able to forget it.

Had we adopted a firmer attitude, explained the situation more clearly, reminded them of our help in the past, shown them clearly what was due from them as Allies, and brought more suggestion of pressure to bear on them, we could have gotten more out of them.

Instead, our attitude has been one of neglect in the earlier stages of the war, then of supplication, flattery and concession, and while the wise ones 'laugh in their sleeve' the ignorant are only encouraged to demand more and more.

How, for instance, can we expect our urgent demands for Naval assistance, shipping, prohibition of imports, etc. to be taken seriously, when the Home papers reek with eulogistic praise of what Japan has (not) done for the Allies.

The policeman (the British Fleet) has been too long absent from his beat, and like small boys, in similar circumstances, the nation has got above itself.

It may be truly said that Japanese nation is drunk with money and dazed with dreams of the leadership of the Pacific.

Sd.

E.H. Rymer,

Captain. R.N.

8/2/18.

Clearly, Japan pursued her national interests in Asia in a manner that conflicted with the British and caused England to distrust her ally. Although the major reason for the dissolution of the Anglo-Japanese Alliance was US pressure (America was afraid that a conflict with Japan in Asia might lead to war with Britain) history tells us that any alliance can easily break down through mutual distrust resulting from perceived inadequate contributions in time of war. The most decisive reason for breaking off the Anglo-Japanese Alliance was that Japan was reluctant to meet a British request for contribution of force for Europe for World War I. An ally should spill blood and sweat when its ally has an emergency. After the Russo-Japanese War, the Japanese Imperial Army was also frustrated: Japan contained the one million-strong Russian Army in Manchuria, whereas the British Army merely stationed 100,000 troops in India and 20,000 in Hong Kong. Therefore, the Japanese Army protected British national interests in India and China with tremendous efforts.

After the September 11 terrorist attack on the US, British Prime Minister Blair came to the US and said, 'My father's generation knew what it was like because they went through the [German] Blitz [during World War II]. There was one country and one people who stood by us at that time, and that country was America and the people was the American people. Just as you stood side by side with us, we stand side by side with you now.' If the Imperial Japanese Government had said during World War I, 'During the Russo-Japanese War, there was one country who helped us side by side. That was the United Kingdom. And this is the time when we will stand side by side to support to UK', the Anglo-Japanese alliance would never have broken off after World War I. Eventually, President Bush announced at the Pearl Harbor commemoration speech on December 7, 2001, 'Today we take special pride that one of our former enemies is now among America's finest friends; we're grateful to our ally, Japan, and to its good people. Today, our two Navies are working side by side in the fight against terror.'[4]

The bilateral alliance between Britain and Japan ended at the Washington Conference in 1921 and Japan joined the Four Power Treaty with the US, Britain, and France, then, later the Nine Power Treaty on China in 1922. Most Japanese at that time thought that the Anglo-Japanese alliance was scrapped for the four-power treaty. However, from these arrangements, the only thing Japan actually received was a delusion of security relations with foreign countries. Japan had to rely heavily on her own military capability to pursue her national interests unilaterally, and then was isolated by America, Britain, Chinese, and Dutch encirclement. Finally, Japan formed an alliance with the wrong country, Hitler's Germany, to avoid isolation. She then went to Pearl Harbor. We do not want to repeat those same failures again. For Japan today, this means that the US–Japan alliance is the fundamental basis for our national security, and multinational security arrangements should not be an alternative measure, but only a supplemental one.

James Przystup wrote in *China, Japan, and the United States*:

> . . . the United States launched the Washington Conference in 1921. The results of the conference, a Four-Power Treaty on the Pacific, a Five-Power Treaty on Naval Limitations, and Nine-Power Treaty on China, established a multilateral cooperative framework for managing the problem of East Asia. . . . To the extent that modern multilateralism contributes to a belief that alliances are passé, it is a security delusion. Neither country should harbor any illusions when it comes to security. The alliance is irreplaceable.

2.   ROME-BERLIN-TOKYO AXIS

This was the worst alliance in which Japan engaged. There was neither trust nor coordination among the partners. For example, after Japan signed the Anti-Comintern Pact with Germany in November 1936, Japan was surprised when Hitler had signed a treaty of nonaggression and friendship with the Soviet Union just three years later. The reaction of the Japanese was unequivocal; they felt that they had been made fools of by Germany. Prime Minister Hiranuma said on resigning the premiership: 'Japan's foreign policy is in a state of having been practically betrayed.'[5] Japan had wanted an alliance as protection against Russia.

Soon after Japan agreed to a neutrality pact with the USSR in April 1941, Japan was again surprised when Hitler attacked the Soviet Union in June 1941. Germany was, in turn, surprised when Japan attacked Pearl Harbor. Lacking trust, neither ally informed the other of its intentions.

Both the Anglo-Japanese Alliance and the Tripartite pact are concrete examples of the balance of power theory. However, the US–Japan alliance is a slightly different case.

3.   THE US–JAPAN RELATIONSHIP

The US–Japan alliance was based on something more than a common threat. It should be remembered that the US–Japan security treaty was signed at the same time as the Peace Treaty in San Francisco. The US incentive to make Japan an alliance partner was not only against the Sino-Soviet alliance of 1950. Additionally, the US Seventh Fleet totally controlled North East Asian regional security. The incentive was that the US never wanted to make Japan an enemy again because of the severe fight in World War II. This was similar to the motivation behind the Anglo-Japanese alliance in which British soldiers were deeply impressed by their Japanese counterparts during the Boxer Rebellion. This alliance means that the US and Japan, which are the great powers on either side of the Pacific Ocean, will never fight each other. This resulted in stability in not only East Asia but also the whole Pacific region, no matter how severe the US–Japan trade dispute would be. Therefore, the US–Japan alliance was not threat-driven but stability-driven.

Walter LaFeber wrote in his book *The Clash*.

> Americans have thus stationed nearly fifty thousand troops and overwhelming naval and air power in and around Japan to protect their foremost economic competitor and help give that competitor easier access to a reassured East and Southeast Asia. Such policies (and ironies) are deeply rooted in and can only be understood in the context of 150 years of US–Japan relations. The differing economic and social systems, competition over China, the US attempts to integrate Japan into the Western system on Western terms, often blatant racism – all go back to the beginnings of the relationship.[6]

The US–Japan relationship has a complex history including close relations in the Meiji Period (1867–1912), bitterness over the Immigration Exclusion Act of 1924, World War II, Japan occupation and, finally, a close partnership. Neither the US nor Japan has such a baggage-laden history with any other country. This history contains negative as well as positive interludes, but the main point is that the US and Japan are today locked in a true partnership, which cannot easily be broken. This is true because it rests on strong support from the people of each nation as public opinion polls continue to indicate. Since both countries are democracies, no government can afford to ignore the will of the people.

4.   COMPARISON WITH THE SINO-SOVIET ALLIANCE

Why, then, did the Sino-Soviet alliance deteriorate so quickly while the US–Japanese alliance persists even to this day? There are many inconsistencies between the Soviet Union and China. First, we have to consider the history of Russia's invasion of Asia in the 15th century. Through territorial treaties between Russia and China, such as the Nerchinsk Treaty of 1689, the Kiakhta Treaty of 1727, the Treaty of Aigun in 1858, the Treaty of Peking in 1860, and the Ili Treaty of 1881, China lost a tremendous amount of territory. This caused great Chinese distrust, first of Russia, then the Soviet Union.

Even during the development period of the Sino-Soviet alliance from 1956 to 1957, the USSR never gave nuclear technology to China. In 1957, Mao Tse-tung made his second trip to Moscow, but his political and economic expectations were unfulfilled. Mao Tse-tung returned to Peking empty-handed, except for the Soviet promise to provide China with mere prototypes of atomic weapons.

Edmund Clubb further contended in *China and Russia* that:

> There was a major difference from what was left unexpressed during that time. In January 1964, Peking viewed Communist 'revisionists' as apostates, and it was evident that China proposed that the 'socialist camp' be composed of itself and those elements of the Communist world who accepted Maoism as the 'True Doctrine.' This separated the so-called 'heretics' from this version of Marxism-Leninism that would, in due course, be classified with the 'imperialists'.[7]

Richard Wich declared in *Sino-Soviet Crisis Politics* that that the Sino-Soviet border crisis was fueled by Peking's perceptions of the Soviet invasion of Czechoslovakia in August 1968. He also professed that, as a result of the Czech invasion, Peking began to formulate a new policy centered on the border issue. This eventually developed into a severe crisis in Sino-Soviet relations. The two major points were:

(1) A new, differentiated and flexible East Europe policy (dramatically illustrated by a rapid rapprochement with Tito), and

(2) A refurbished East Asian Policy, consisting of an openness to a negotiated settlement in Vietnam (a significant departure) and an overture to the incoming Nixon administration.[8]

While Moscow has transferred weapons technology to China since World War II, they have never given critical or advanced technologies. Nelsen Harvey declared in *Power and Insecurity: Beijing, Moscow and Washington 1949–1988* that 'the interactions of the three powers were determined by national security concerns, and that some shifts in policy or crises may be explained by initial threats, subsequent over-reaction, and escalation.' He concludes that the main source of Sino-Soviet tension was strategic in nature, and Sino-Soviet relations must viewed through their respective relations with the US.[9]

Robert E. Osgood listed as the first reason why the Sino-Soviet Alliance fell apart was that the historically familiar contest for power and prestige between two ambitious nations of sufficient independence from each other permitted active competition.[10] The US–Japan alliance persisted because America and Japan share the same values of freedom and democracy as well as market economics. Militarily, both nations are interdependent. Japan relies upon the US nuclear umbrella and offensive capability, which Japan cannot possess due to her Constitution. Simultaneously, the US relies upon forward bases in Japan and host nation support. Both countries enjoy economic prosperity through trade based on their firm security relationship.

In conclusion, China and the Soviet Union had many disagreements, while the US and Japan share the same values and have an interdependent relationship. Since the 15ᵗʰ century, when China lost much territory to Russia, there remained an atmosphere of severe distrust. Similarly, the Soviets feared that China would someday seek revenge for its loss of territory. Furthermore, the USSR worried because China had a much greater population compared to the Soviets in the Asian-Pacific region. Militarily, the Soviets and China were independent, both having nuclear weapons. Even though the Soviets and China were in the Communist camp, they did not necessarily share the same goals.

NOTES

[1] Charles W. Kegley, Jr., and Gregory A. Raymond, *When Trust Breaks Down,* University of South Carolina 1990, p. 182

[2] *The Modality of the Security and Defense Capability of Japan,* Advisory Group on Defense Issues, Aug. 12 1994

[3] Doc. 119 [46022], *Japan at War 1914–19–,* (From Capt. R.E. Rymer to Admiralty, 11 March 1918), FO. 371-3233. Public Record Office London

[4] President Bush's speech in Norfolk, Virginia, December 7 during ceremonies aboard the U.S.S. *Enterprise* marking the 60th anniversary of the Japanese attack on Pearl Harbor in 2001

[5] Fairbank, Reischauer, Craig, *East Asia The Modern Transformation,* Houghton Mifflin Company, 1965, p. 607

[6] Walter LaFeber, *The Clash; US–Japan relations throughout history,* W.W. Norton & Company, 1997

[7] O. Edmund Clubb, *China & Russia,* Columbia University Press, 1971, p. 467

[8] Richard Wich, *Sino-Soviet Crisis Politics,* Council on East Asia Studies, Harvard University, 1980

[9] Nelsen Harvey W., *Power and Insecurity: Beijing, Moscow, and Washington 1948–1988,* Boulder, CO, Lynn Rienner, 1989

[10] Robert E. Osgood, *Alliance and American Foreign Policy,* The Johns Hopkins Press, 1968, p. 110

3

The US–Japan Alliance Rationale for Japan

A public opinion poll in Japan, which was taken in November 1997, indicated that the most reliable country for Japan was the US. About 40 percent of Americans, and 68 percent of Japanese wanted the US to be Japan's alliance partner in the 21st century.

No official publication, such as the Japan Defense White Paper or the Diplomatic Blue Paper clearly states Japan's national interests, yet most would agree that it must be the survival and prosperity of the country. In reviewing Japan's natural factors – territory smaller than the state of California; large population, almost half that of the US; few natural resources; and surrounded by the sea – Japan has only a few options to pursue survival and prosperity. In the Imperialist era, one of the options was to expand her territory and obtain natural resources by using military force. In the modern era, however, the only option is to become a trading state[1] through the sea lines of communication. Considering its geographic environment, Japan's strategy to pursue her national interests must be: (1) to maintain a friendly relationship with maritime nations, especially those with strong naval powers; (2) to avoid isolation; and (3) to maintain a stable and secure world. Looking back at Japanese history, the period where Japan was involved on the Asian continent was an unhappy one, whereas the period where Japan enjoyed free trade via the oceans was a prosperous one. We will analyze the US–Japan alliance rationale through the above perspective.

1. GEOPOLITICAL PERSPECTIVE

A wise strategist once observed that, 'everything changes but geography.' My own philosophy is that island or peninsula countries should be allied together in this modern industrial age. On the ocean, transportational direction is free so that transportational power and volume are vast, whereas transportational direction on land is restricted by terrain such as mountains and rivers so that transportational power of land networks including rail, is far less than ships' transportational power. Therefore, island and peninsular countries should be tied with maritime nations.

It seems that there are three kinds of distances: real distance, elapsed time distance and transportation distance. To illustrate, let's compare the distance to Yosemite National Park (in central California), Omaha Nebraska (in the middle of the US), and Tokyo from San Francisco (northern California). The nearest place in 'real distance' is Yosemite (about four hours' drive). In 'time distance' however, Omaha is the closest, because we can travel by air (about three hours by air). But when we carry a million tons of wheat, Tokyo is the nearest due to ships' 'transportation' capacity and thereby cost-effectiveness. In this modern industrial era, we have heavily depended upon sea routes for transportation. Almost 90 percent of total shipping has gone by sea because it is cost-effective. In this sense, the US is closer to Japan than to China or Russia. Furthermore, the world has been connected by computer-based electronic links, such as the Internet, as well as by video-telecommunication. In this regard, the US is much closer to Japan than to China or Russia because of the computer-based electronic infrastructure. Even when Manchuria was Japanese territory, Japan imported most timbers from the US and not from northern Manchuria which it is geographically much closer to than the American continent because of the transportation cost.

Island or peninsula countries like Japan and Italy are trading nations who make their living by commerce. Therefore, they rely on maritime-based transportation in order to survive. They need to be allied with strong sea/naval powers such as the UK or the US.

History shows good and bad examples in the Anglo-Japanese Alliance from 1902 to 1921 and the Italian alliance in World War I. Italy in the World War I was initially allied with the land powers, Germany and Austria-Hungary; however, Italy could not secure its access to the vital resource of coal. As the British and the French, maritime superpowers in the Mediterranean Sea, became hostile, Italy had to drop out of its alliance with the land powers. Japan's biggest mistake in modern diplomatic history was breaking off the Anglo-Japanese alliance, as I explained previously. History tells us that Japan has enjoyed prosperous periods when she allied with maritime nations such as Britain and the US comparing unhappy periods when Japan had ties with land powers, such as Russia in 1916 during World War I, with China in 1918 for sending troops to Siberia, and with Germany from 1940 to the end of World War II. Today, Japan's first priority in national security policy is the maintenance of sound security relations with the US, which remains a naval superpower. Thus, island and peninsula countries must cooperate together. In this sense, an East Asian Community initiated on the 8th ASEAN + 3 Summit in November 2004, is questionable for Japanese prosperity. In the Jan/Feb 2000 *Foreign Affairs*, Former Under Secretary of State, Robert B. Zoellick wrote an article about the potential alliance between the US (naval superpower), Japan (island), ROK (peninsula), and Australia (island).[2] This idea represents the same context, which is elaborated above.

If the Korean peninsula will ultimately be unified, a unified Korea should be aligned with the major maritime nations. Modern industrial states, which import raw materials and export industrial products, must survive through open sea lines of communication. A unified Korea would never oppose the strongest naval power, the US, as well as the Asian naval power, Japan. This alliance should be bonded together by the Navy.

The US–Japan alliance, for example, is sometimes called Navy Alliance. It is true that the alliance is based upon a strong Navy-to-Navy relationship. Among the three services, the Japan Maritime Self-Defense Force and US Navy relationship is the strongest. Looking at current issues, which I will discuss in Chapter 6, the review of Guidelines for Japan-US Defense Cooperation (Guidelines) and Ballistic Missile Defense (BMD) are mainly Navy related issues, as is Maritime Intercept

Operations (MIO), Mine Sweeping Operations, Search and Rescue (SAR) at Sea, Noncombatant Evacuation Operations (NEO), and Navy theater-wide technical cooperation. After the September 11 terrorist attack, Japan Maritime Self-Defense Force ships supported US and coalition naval combatants in the Northern Arabian Sea. In April 2002, Admiral Toru Ishikawa, the Chief of Maritime Staff, addressed at the 50th anniversary ceremony of the Japan Maritime Self-Defense Force, 'The US–Japan alliance is what we call "Maritime Alliance" that unites the two Pacific Nations.'[3]

2.   THE COLD WAR IS NOT COMPLETELY OVER IN ASIA

Michael Yahuda argued in his book *The International Politics of the Asia-Pacific, 1945–1995*, that 'the Cold War is not over in the Asia-Pacific.' He stated: 'China, which, unlike the Soviet Union, was spared the pressures in the 1970s because of its value as an ally against the Soviet Union and in the 1980s because it was believed to be embarked on a more liberal road, has been the main target of American human rights concerns since the Tiananmen killings of 4 June 1989.'[4] Robert S. Ross warned in *New World: American Grand Strategy in the Post-Cold War Era* that continued tension, reduced economic and military cooperation, US continued criticism of Chinese human rights abuses and policies attempting to modify China's behavior could backfire.[5] Richard Bernstein and Ross Munro also argued in their book *The Coming Conflict with China*, that economic growth now offers China the means to challenge US hegemony. Therefore, China will seek to displace the US in East Asia, resulting in hostile long-term rivalry.[6]

It is true that the Cold War is not fully over in Asia. The Cold War structure itself went away in 1989, but there are still four communist countries in Asia, namely China, North Korea, Vietnam and Laos. Additionally, the Taiwan-China and the North and South Korea standoff, with almost two million armed personnel, remain major concerns in the region. A Japanese-Russian Peace Treaty from World War II has not been affected due to the unresolved Northern Territories dispute. Therefore, Japanese security concerns today include: uncertainty regarding the Korean Peninsula, especially the development of long-range ballistic missiles and nuclear weapons by the North Koreans; Chinese naval expansion and the strengthening of her maritime presence in areas of territorial disputes; and the military power remaining in Russia's Far East area. These lingering concerns will continue during the next decade because, for example, Korean unification is not likely over the horizon. The Chinese ballistic missile development and naval as well as air force modernization will continue. Russian uncertainty will remain. Therefore, the US–Japan Security Treaty is essential for Japan's national security. Even if the above Japanese security concerns are relieved in the near future, US - Japanese security relations are still necessary for regional stability to suppress weapons proliferation and regional conflicts.

3.   NO OTHER OPTIONS TO SECURE JAPAN

If the US–Japan Alliance ends, there would appear to be three other options for Japan to ensure its security: first, to build up unilateral capabilities including nuclear weapons; second, enter a bilateral alliance with a land power such as China and/or Russia; and third, resort to multilateral forums/cooperation.

It is obvious that the second and third options are unfeasible due to various reasons, which we have already discussed above. Japan does not share the same values of freedom and democracy with Russia and China. Additionally, a Chinese and Russian nuclear umbrella would be unreliable to Japan. There are some who insist Japan should join with Asian nations rather than the US. This option is unacceptable for not only geopolitical reasons, which I stated previously, but also military, economic, and political reasons. Regarding a multilateral framework, reliance on the United Nations is still premature in the current global climate. The UN does not have any standing military forces which means that it cannot conduct coercive action alone. It is also premature to rely on a multinational security framework in East Asia. Despite the fact that the Asian Pacific Regional Forum has been growing recently, they also do not have coercive military power if some invasion should occur. It is important, however, to develop confidence-building measures through various exchange programs, including military ones.

Finally, we have to discuss unilateral capabilities. Even though every country wants to make their own defense decisions, the autonomous defense policy is out of date. It is also impossible to build up sufficient unilateral capabilities because the Japanese period of peak economic growth has passed. *New World Coming: American Security in the 21st Century* by the United States Commission on National Security for the 21st Century in 1999, stated that:

> It is not hard to see the predicates for a 'go it alone' scenario in Tokyo, even through, on balance, it is not very likely to occur. It could go something like this. Under the best of circumstances, Japan's share of global GDP will have dropped from about 8 percent in the late 1990s to roughly 4.5 percent by 2025. For a political culture that has based its self-image almost exclusively on economic success since 1946, this is not good news.[7]

The baby boom generation in Japan, now in their fifties, will reach retirement age in the next generation, thereby greatly adding to the cultural and fiscal pressures associated with the aging of Japanese society. Since Japan has the longest average life-span in the world, a smaller number of people will have to support a much larger pool of older people. By 2010 to 2015, a quarter of the population will be sixty-five years of age or older and every two Japanese in the working population (those fifteen to sixty-four) will have to support one person of sixty-five years or older. In 2005, Japan's population started to decline. Yet the Japanese government total debt is 1000 trillion yen (about $9 trillion, which is about twice the country's annual GDP), requiring an interest payment of about 20 trillion yen per year – an amount which is almost the same as the social security payments. The Japanese budget deficit and national debt are among the worst among major industrial democracies, rapidly approaching those of Italy. Japan could not meet the Maastricht EMU criteria for ratio of deficit to GDP or the amount of debt relative to GDP.[8] In addition, the continuous economic recession in Japan has created both domestic and international pressures for a reduction in income tax. Consequently, Japan will face increasing financial difficulty in the next couple of decades. Hence, economic power – Japan's only source of real power – will diminish over the next generation.

The Japanese population is aging faster than that of other

industrial countries. Just as important is the fact that the total fertility rate (births per woman) is about 1.3, which is among the lowest in the world and seems to be falling further. Japanese demographic trends influence military strength. The male population within the ages eligible for recruitment into the SDF is sharply declining.[9] Japanese SDF manpower will never increase as long as the Japanese government pursues a volunteer military system. The government has no choice, though, because Japan interprets conscription as being unconstitutional. Notwithstanding that legal point, the draft system itself is completely out of date and unacceptable for today's professional military. Based on the fifteen NATO countries in 1988, volunteer system countries were only four (USA, Canada, Luxembourg, and UK). By 2003 the number had grown to eight (now including Belgium, France, Netherlands, and Spain), and is ten in 2006 (adding Italy and Portugal). One of worst mistakes Japan made when it began World War II was overestimating its own national power. In the future, a proper estimate of Japan's national power is essential. In conclusion, Japan should not develop an autonomous defense policy.

Additionally, there are two constraints for Japanese security policy – geopolitical and historical. Regarding the geopolitical constraint, there are four countries in close proximity to Japan out of the five who have more than a million troops in the world; the US, Russia, China, and North Korea. Historically, Japan was defeated in World War II. Therefore, there are no other options to ensure Japan's security except by alliance. The question is which country should Japan ally with: the US, Russia, or China. Russia's GDP is only less than one fifth of Japan's. China does not share the same democratic values as Japan. In order to enjoy democracy and prosperity through free trade, the only acceptable option is an alliance with the US.

4.   JAPANESE VULNERABILITY

Robert Keohane and Joseph S. Nye stated in *Power and Interdependence*:

> All countries were significantly vulnerable to a catastrophe . . . To understand the role of power in interdependence, we must distinguish between dimensions, *sensitivity* and *vulnerability*. . . . An

example of sensitivity dependence is the way the United States, Japan, and Western Europe were affected by increased oil prices in 1971 and again in 1973–74 . . . Two countries, each importing 35 percent of their petroleum needs, may seem equally sensitive to price rises; but if one could shift to domestic sources at moderate cost, and the other had no such alternative, the second state would be more *vulnerable* than the first. The vulnerability dimension of interdependence rests on the relative availability and costliness of the alternatives that various actors face . . . sensitivity interdependence will be less important than vulnerability interdependence in providing power resources to actors. [10]

Japan has a great number of vulnerabilities that must be overcome in order to sustain her survival and prosperity. Economically, Japan depends on necessary resources, such as oil, minerals, and food.

Militarily, Japan has to rely on the nuclear umbrella and offensive capabilities of its alliance partner, the US, because of its constitutional restrictions. Moreover, Japan's Self-Defense Forces have relied on the US Armed Forces for their exercise ranges and for critical information sharing. For example, the Japan Ground Self-Defense Force uses the training ranges in Tacoma, Washington; the Maritime Self-Defense Force uses the Pacific Missile Range in Hawaii; and the Air Self-Defense Force uses the Missile Range in El Paso, Texas. This is because Japan does not have adequate exercise or missile ranges.

In 1991, George Friedman and Meredith LeBard captured global attention with their book, *The Coming War with Japan.*[11] Former Secretary of Defense Caspar Weinberger co-authored a book entitled *The Next War*, in which conflict against Japan is one of the next war scenarios.[12] According to this book, economic conflict between Japan and the US escalates as US economic sanctions are imposed against Japan, and in 2007 Japan invades Brunei to get oil. In a practical sense, however, even though the Japanese armed forces have been equipped extensively with US weapons, to include AEGIS ships, P-3C, F-15 and AWACS aircraft, and Patriot missiles, the US has retained a large database and source codes. Without American technology, Japan SDF could not catch up to a world top-level capability. For this reason, it would be implausible to believe that Japan would fight with the US.

Japan Self-Defense Forces have been sending Peace Keeping Operations (PKO) units all over the world, but mainly rely on the US for necessary intelligence because Japan does not possess a global information collection system such as satellite surveillance. This is not only the case with PKO but American sources are relied upon today for all vital information regarding military threats. In this sense, the US provides not only a nuclear umbrella but also an information umbrella. Joseph S. Nye, Jr., and William A. Owens stated in *America's Information Edge*, 'Just as nuclear dominance was the key to coalition leadership in the old era, information dominance will be the key in the information age.'[13] During my tour as Defense and Naval Attaché to the Embassy of Japan in Washington DC from 1996 to 1999, I strongly recognized that we could not undertake any military operation without US information support. In August 1996, a large portion of the Syrian Army began unusual movements. If Syria intended to launch a surprise attack against Israel, Japanese PKO forces in the Golan Heights could be overrun. The US Defense Intelligence Agency (DIA) estimated that the Syrian Army movement was a routine reposition of forces and not one intended to attack Israel. This information made the Japanese Government decide to keep its PKO troops in the Golan Heights.

Japan's national security concerns have become so global that Japan must pay attention to the incidents literally on the other side of the world. For example, if the Persian Gulf and/or Kosovo situations become truly serious, the US aircraft carrier battle group and/or amphibious readiness groups stationed in Japan would possibly swing to those regions. Consequently, Japan's security environment becomes less stable. Therefore, accurate intelligence of the Gulf and/or European theater is very critical for Japan's security, too. Regarding Non-combatant Evacuation Operations (NEO), timely information is also very critical, because early initiation of NEO could make the situation worse, and late action is equally dangerous. During the Cambodian crisis of July 1997 and Indonesian crisis of May 1998, the Japanese Government depended heavily on US intelligence. *The United States and Japan: Advancing Toward a Mature Partnership*, Institute for National Strategic Studies Special Report in October 2000, emphasized that both within and beyond Asia, Japan faces more diverse threats and more complex international responsibilities, which call for intelligence that provides a better understanding of its national security needs.[14] In addition to intelligence, actual NEO forces are also provided to Japanese citizens abroad in many cases. For example, when states fail (Albania in March 1997, Sierra Leone, Guinea Bissau, and Ethiopia-Eritrea from 1998 to 1999) the Japanese Government must ask for NEO assistance, because Japan has a legal restriction as well as limited capability to conduct its own NEO.

Should the US–Japan alliance break down, Japan must create the above assets on its own. In November 1996, in an article in the *Bungei Shunju*, the Democratic Party leader, Mr Hatoyama, articulated a vision of 'A Security Treaty Without Stationing Troops During Peacetime.'[15] In his essay, Hatoyama acknowledged the importance of the role of the US–Japan security relationship, but addressed in greater detail the necessity of promoting multinational regional forums. He proposed that a comprehensive review of the US–Japan Security Treaty be conducted, with the aim of removing US forces on Okinawa and mainland Japan by the year 2010 while concurrently concluding a US–Japan free-trade agreement. Former Japanese Prime Minister Morihiro Hosokawa also wrote an article, 'Are US Troops in Japan Needed?' in *Foreign Affairs*.[16] In this article, he insisted that it was time for Americans to go home. This was a 'no-bases alliance' option, with which the newly-formed Democratic Party briefly experimented. I have seen similar arguments in many Japanese books such as *The Japan That Can say No* written by Shintaro Ishihara and Akio Morita. However, those people understand neither Japan's particular vulnerability, which I mentioned above, nor that the US–Japan alliance has a give and take component in which the US will defend Japan and Japan provides forward bases and host nation support for the US military.

Article 5 of the treaty of Mutual Cooperation and Security between Japan and the US states that each party recognizes that an armed attack against either Party in the territories under the administration of Japan would be dangerous to its own peace and safety, and declares that it would act to meet the common danger in accordance with its constitutional provisions and process. Article 6 states that for the purpose of contributing to the security of Japan and the maintenance of international peace and security in the Far East, the US is granted the use by its land, air and naval forces of facilities and areas in Japan. The Ishihara camp also overestimated the Japan Self-Defense Force capability. For example, the only possible method to defend Japan from North Korean ballistic missile threat at this time is a US preemptive strike on North Korean, because the Ballistic Missile Defense (BMD) system is not yet ready. Therefore, US Navy ships with Tomahawk cruise missiles or a carrier air wing and the US Air Force F-16s in Misawa are an essential element to deterring North Korea. If those American troops were sent home as Mr Hosokawa insisted, it would take several weeks to deploy them to this region. North Korea's strategy is to finish the war rapidly because they know that they will lose the war if it is prolonged. Therefore, it will be too late if American forces are not forward deployed to Japan. Why should we ask America to pull this essential element for our defense out of Japan? Morally, it takes a great deal for granted for Japan to say: 'We do not want American Bases in Japan but please come and defend us in an emergency anyway.' I am personally afraid that the Americans, especially Congress, will say: 'O.K., we will abandon our bases in Japan but we will no longer purchase Japanese goods. And, we will no longer defend Japan either.'

The Governor of Tokyo, Shintaro Ishihara, insists on the joint use of Yokota Air Base with Japanese civilian activities, and calculates an enormous economic benefit in joint use. Even US scholars like Paul Giarra, for example, endorse Governor Ishihara's position. Paul Giarra stated that on the Kanto Plain, for example, Yokota Air Base could be developed as a major civil air cargo hub for Tokyo, while preserving its basic logistical functions and vital surge capacity for the US Air Force. Civil access to Atsugi Air Base could help relieve some of the severe pressure directed at that combined SDF-US forces base.[17] However, they overlook the necessary expansion during wartime. Though Yokota Air Base may not look so busy in peacetime, it could potentially be tremendously busy during a regional conflict. During the situation in Kosovo, for example, Aviano Air Base in Italy expanded its capacity seven times when compared to peacetime usage. The average sortie rate during peacetime was 240 per week, whereas 240 sorties per day were flown from Aviano during the Kosovo operation. It will expand logistic 'tails' such as fuel, ammunition, mainte-nance, and supply, as well. The US bases appear to have excess space when compared with the surrounding high-density civil-ian population areas. However, this is only peacetime. If the US Air Mobility Command (AMC) were to request the use of Narita or Haneda airports during any conflict situation in the area sur-rounding Japan, the Japanese government would probably reject this outright because of political reasons. The Japanese government made a commitment to the Japanese that these airports would have no military purpose. Therefore, the only airport available in the Kanto Plain for airlift purpose is Yokota Air Base. If Governor Ishihara requests Yokota Air Base for dual use, he should accept Haneda airport for military purposes during any emergency.

During the earthquake exercise in September 2001, how-ever, Yokota Air Force base opened for Japanese rescue aircraft. Similarly, Sagamihara US Army supply depot, for example, will create field and general hospitals to treat about 2000 patients during wartime. Those capabilities might be available for Japanese people in the case of humanitarian rescue opera-tions, including earthquakes. When, as the President of Joint Staff College in 2001, I had discussions with Major General Alan D. Johnson, the Commanding General US Army Japan at Camp Zama, he proposed the idea to let the Japan Ground Self-Defense Force Engineering Corps – also stationed in Camp Zama – learn how to construct those field and general hospitals so that they could establish those facilities by them-selves during major natural disasters in Japan. These uses of Yokota and Sagamihara bases are typical examples of interde-pendence between the US and Japanese during major natural disasters.

Nationalistic approaches, in which foreign bases are closed in Japan, are becoming obsolete in these interdependent times. In fact, there are so many American factories, indus-tries, and companies in Japan, that the significance of terri-tory in the context of the world system is becoming vague.

In conclusion, Japan's defense capability is so vulnerable and interdependent with the US that Japan must continue the alliance with America in the future.

NOTES

[1] Richard Rosecrance, *The Rise of the Trading State*, Basic Books, 1986

[2] Robert B. Zoellick, *A Republican Foreign Policy*, Foreign Affairs of January/February 2000, pp. 74–75

[3] Admiral Toru Ishikawa, Address on the 50th anniversary of the Japan Maritime Self-Defense Force at Yokosuka, April 26, 2002

[4] Michael Yahuda *The International Politics of the Asia-Pacific, 1945–1995*, Routledge, 1996, p. 280

[5] Robert S. Ross, *A New World: American Grand Strategy in the Post-Cold War Era*

[6] Richard Bernstein and Ross Munro, *The Coming Conflict with China*, New York: Knopf, 1997

[7] The United States Commission on National Security 21st Century, *New World Coming: American Security in the 21st century*, September 15 1999

[8] Koji Watanabe, *Japan in Need of Reform and Trilateralism*, The Trilateral Commission, July 1997

[9] *Defense of Japan 1997*, Defense Agency, p. 182 Diagram 4–14; Changes in Male Population at the Ages Eligible for Recruitment of Privates (GSDF), Seamen Apprentice (MSDF) and Airmen 3rd Class (ASDF)

[10] Robert Keohane and Joseph S. Nye, *Power and Interdependence*, Boston 1989, pp. 8, 11–13, 15

[11] George Friedman and Meredith LeBard, *The Coming War with Japan*, New York: St Martins, 1991

[12] Caspar Weinberger & Peter Schweizer, *The Next War*, 1996

[13] Joseph S. Nye, Jr., and William A. Owens, *America's Information Edge*, Foreign Affairs, Vol. 75, No. 2, March/April 1996, p. 27

[14] *The United States and Japan: Advancing Toward a Mature Partnership*, Institute for National Strategic Studies National Defense Studies, October 2000, p. 5

[15] *Political Platform of DPJ's Hatoyama Noted*, FBIS-EAS-96-203, November 1, 1996

[16] Morihiro Hosokawa, 'Are US Troops in Japan Needed?,' *Foreign Affairs*, July/August 1998 Volume 77, Number 4, pp. 2–5

[17] Paul S. Giarra, *US Bases in Japan: Historical Background and Innovative Approaches*, The Council on Foreign Relations, 1999, p. 137

4

The US–Japan Alliance Rationale for the US

According to the 1998 US Image of Japan Study prepared by the Gallup Organization, close to half of all Americans express no opinion about Japan as a country, but among those who do, opinion remains favorable by a margin of roughly three to one, 41 percent to 12 percent. The most commonly cited reasons for having a favorable view of Japan are cultural or having to do with the perceived personal qualities of the Japanese people. A high regard for Japan's technology also emerges as an important contributor to positive US impressions of Japan. Negative impressions of Japan, by contrast, are driven almost equally by two major factors: trade/economic relations with the US and general political relations with the US. The perception that Japan is a dependable ally of the US remains positive at a two-to-one ratio, 60 percent to 27 percent. The 1998 study records very slight increases in support for the US–Japan Mutual Security Treaty over 1997, both in terms of the extent to which Americans believe the treaty contributes to stability in Asia, and in terms of support for maintaining the treaty. Public support for maintaining the treaty is somewhat higher in 1998 than it was in 1996 (83 percent vs. 75 percent).

According to *A National Security Strategy For A New Century* which was published by the White House in December 1999, the US national security strategy consists of three core objectives: first, to enhance American's security; second, to bolster American's economic prosperity; and third, to promote democracy and human rights abroad.[1] In the context of those three strategies, the US–Japan alliance is critical for American national interests for three primary reasons. First, forward military bases in Japan are necessary to help maintain global security, especially two potential theaters of war – one on the Korean Peninsula and one in the Middle East. Second, the US and Japanese GDP combined account for about 45 percent of the total world economy. Japanese economic power is essential to promote US prosperity, and therefore, there is no reason to terminate the alliance relation with Japan. In fact, there is every reason to maintain it. Finally, Japan is the most democratic country in East Asia. For these reasons above, the American Congress should continue to be interested in the US–Japan Mutual Security Treaty.

More specifically, US interests in Asia as defined by Richard J. Samuels and Christopher P. Twomey are as follows:

(1) Preserving stability among the great powers.
(2) Preserving the safety of the sea-lanes of communication (SLOCs) throughout East and Southeast Asia.
(3) Maintaining an American leadership role in regional and global institutions.
(4) Peaceful resolution of the division of the Korean Peninsula on Seoul's terms.
(5) Peaceful resolution of the Chinese-Taiwan conflict that upholds democracy and economic freedom.
(6) Avoiding the proliferation of weapons of mass destruction (WMD).
(7) Ensuring the independence of Indochina and Southeast Asia.

Samuels and Twomey stated that neither isolationism nor multilateralism – supported by some in the public debate today – will achieve the American goals laid out above.[2] The US wants to engage Asian countries economically. Therefore, stability in the region is critical for the American security strategy. In order to maintain necessary stability in Asia, the US must maintain its forward bases to ensure access to the region.

Reviewing the US security policy in Asia, there are several options; Unilateralism, bilateralism, and multilateralism. These will be investigated more closely below.

1.   UNILATERALISM; ISOLATIONISM

(a)   Consistent streams of thought or ideological impulse behind American isolationism
The origin of American isolationism is seen in George Washington's farewell address in 1796, in which he clarified the 'great rule of conduct' regarding American foreign policy. Washington cautioned that the newly independent United States should:

> Minimize political relations with foreign countries on developing overseas trade. Especially Europe, to relate with them as minimum as possible, because US interests would conflict or have no relation with European countries' interest. Oppose establishing alliance relations with foreign countries except temporary ones during a crisis.

This became the foundation for American foreign policy until the twentieth century.

Like George Washington's farewell address, Thomas Jefferson's inauguration speech advocated avoiding formal relations with other countries, by encouraging 'peace, commerce and honest friendship with all nations, entangling alliances with none.' This means that it is better for the US, a new country on the world stage, to continue internal development and not become involved in external European struggles.

This policy stems both from consideration for self-preservation by a newly independent nation and the idea that the new republic should remain aloof from the politics of the Old World. The latter point had a lot to do with American nationalism, which emphasized that the new nation was better and morally superior to the old European ones. Isolationism was closely tied to American nationalism and was deeply rooted in the young American psyche.

The US is geographically detached from the European continent. The Atlantic Ocean is a 'natural barrier,' as C. Van Woodward stated, against European influence both politically and militarily. Therefore, for America, the importance of military power and diplomacy remained limited for much of its early history.

The US possessed vast resources in its own territory, and therefore early in its history it did not have to rely heavily on resources from overseas countries. This enabled the US to maintain its isolationist policy.

American isolationism can be divided into two parts. One is unilateralism which was applied to the Western Hemisphere, and the other was non-interventionism which was applied to its policy *vis-à-vis* Europe.

The Monroe Doctrine of 1823 not only was a guarantee to Latin America that no European power would subjugate the continent, but it was an equally clear statement that Washington regarded the region as its own sphere of influence, where America security concerns were to be respected by all parties. With the Monroe Doctrine, the US had declared itself opposed to the reimposition of European rule in the Western Hemisphere and so aligned itself with nationalist forces in Latin America, whose states Washington would recognize as sovereign.

After the Spanish-American War, the US maintained its isolationist policy even though America's sphere of influence expanded. It was, however, not a matter of American obtaining colonies that would cause conflict with other major powers – it was the isolationist policy itself.

During World War I, the US maintained its neutrality until 1917, when isolationism was no longer a rational policy due to the dramatically changing international situation. However, US participation in World War I was thought by some to be not necessarily against isolationism, because the US had reacted to a direct threat. After World War I, the US opposed ratification for the Versailles Treaty, as well as participation in the League of Nations.

President Woodrow Wilson's internationalism was indeed a departure from the isolationist tradition. In fact, it stemmed partly from this very isolationist tradition. Isolationists attempted to keep the new order in the Western Hemisphere intact by keeping America away from the Old World. American internationalists, however, sought to actually impose their new order on the Old World.

From 1919 to 1941, some argue that America's inter-war isolationism had changed; others argued that it was intact, consistent with that before the war. Orthodox theory is that

American behavior was based upon justice, and her entry into World War I was a temporary aberration. Realist theory holds that US policy during World War I was confused because of its moralistic approach. But the US could have a realistic perspective during the inter-war period. Therefore, realists insisted that American isolationism had actually changed. The New Left, however, argued that American isolationism had not changed at all because American foreign policy consistently sought to gain an economic benefit from abroad, including the 'Open Door' policy and taking advantage of war.

In 1918, Wilsonian idealism and internationalism characterized American foreign policy. After 1921, however, the narrower nationalism and isolationism of the Republican administrations of Warren G. Harding, Calvin Coolidge, and Herbert Hoover replaced Wilsonian liberalism. For example, this insular vision was embodied in the Johnson Act of 1924, which sharply curtailed immigration. Congress excluded from entry to the US all Orientals ineligible for citizenship under American law. Selig Adler wrote in *The Uncertain Giant: 1921–1941*, 'Internationalists were stymied by three factors: first; they couldn't support the League, second; they lacked the support of either major party, and third; senators from the isolationist hinterland would block internationalism'.[3] Robert Davis Johnson stated in *The Peace Progressive and American Foreign Relations*, 'From 1919–1930, a few key senators, Congressmen, public officials, and social leaders were seeking domestic, progressive programs. In doing so, they opposed entanglements with Western Europe.' Johnson explains the 1920's isolationism as a product of these men.[4] On the other hand, Melvyn P. Leffler argued in *Open Door Expansion, World Order, and Democratic Constraint*, 'It is not true that this period was characterized by isolation. American officials sought to join the World Court, sign arbitration treaties, outlaw war, and protect property.'[5]

World War I left the US with the strong sentiment that American should never again be involved in war in Europe. This sentiment was crystallized in the 1930 Neutrality Act. According to Dr Irie of Harvard University, Franklin Delano Roosevelt (FDR)'s Good Neighbor Policy in 1933 represented isolationism, because FDR wanted to keep the Western

Hemisphere apart from Europe and Asia. In this context, another Neutrality Act came into force in 1935, banning the sale and delivery of armaments to belligerent countries. This Act deprived FDR of the authority to use arms embargoes, as sanctions against Axis powers. Moreover, in 1936, another Neutrality Act became law prohibiting the provision of loans to belligerent countries. These two acts prevented FDR from exercising any positive influence upon European affairs.

Republican ascendancy declined in the aftermath of the Wall Street collapse of 1929 and was replaced in 1933 by FDR's Democratic administration. Thus began a new era in American foreign policy that was circumscribed by the increasing isolation of the US and codified in neutrality legislation that sought carefully to protect American external interests and security in an ever-more dangerous world.

Wayne Cole argued in *Roosevelt and the Isolationism, 1932–1945*:

> Isolationist opinion played heavily on the President, as it did on Hull and others, in furthering and shielding what they reckoned to be American external interests. FDR was an internationalist who had to align himself with isolationist legislators in his first term to ensure the passage of critical New Deal domestic legislation. By FDR's second term, the alliance with isolationists, never firm, had weakened because of perceived external threats to American strategic interests, particularly Europe. Therefore, FDR's Foreign Policy by 1941 was constrained by isolationism. Then after his election to the third term, and with the outbreak of war in Europe, FDR worked assiduously to destroy isolationism as a political force by any means possible. The destruction of isolationism as a credible force within American domestic politics after 1941, doggedly sought by FDR, helped pave the way for American rise as a world leader.[6]

It became increasingly difficult for the US to continue its isolationistic policy during the 1930s because of the emerging threat from Germany and Japan. However, the Great Depression made the US focus inward. Even though the US could not fully maintain its isolationism from 1934 to 1937, it was clear that the American people favored this view. Finally, in 1941, America abandoned this policy due to the

French surrender to the Nazis and the Japanese attack on Pearl Harbor.

Manfred Jonas argued in *Isolationism in America, 1935–1941*:

> Why isolationism disappeared in 1939 was the result of Hitler's and Japan's war mongering that could not keep the US out or maintain its unilateralism. Because isolationists were also realists, once Hitler and Japan attacked, there was no room for the US unilateral action. Only alliance making war could prevent Axis domination of the world. Because of this structural change, isolationism disappeared, at least in the form of 1930s isolationism.[7]

World War II proved that American isolationism was inadequate to prevent war from reaching America's shores. Wilsonian internationalism was thus revived and NATO was formed in 1949 as the first alliance for the US during peacetime.

Following the Korean War, isolationistic views such as 'Fortress America' reemerged. President Truman, however, persuaded the American people to keep an internationalist outlook by raising the specter of the Munich syndrome. Through the Great Debate in the Senate in 1951, bipartisan consensus for US international commitments was obtained.

(b)   Distinction between Asia/Pacific and Europe

Robert Tucker argued in *A New Isolationism*, 'American isolationism has co-existed with expansionism. Even though the US is isolated, she expanded her territory in the Continent and also expanded her sphere of influence in the Western Hemisphere as well as East Asia.'[8] During the debate on the 'Open Door' policy from 1893 to 1901, pragmatic expansionists represented by President McKinley, Secretary of State John Hay, and many entrepreneurs and lawyers insisted that the US should annex certain Pacific islands that were deemed militarily and economically important, and call for free trade through the 'Open-Door' in China. After the Spanish-American War, the US aggressively expanded her sphere of influence in Asia by annexing the Philippines, Hawaii and Guam, as well as Puerto Rico through the resulting peace treaty. In 1899, John Hay announced the Open-Door policy and the US resolved to actively protect its interests in China.

During the Russo-Japanese War, President Theodore Roosevelt mediated the end of the conflict and maintained the balance of power in Asia through the resulting Portsmouth Treaty. Consequently, he was awarded the Nobel Prize for Peace. The US and Japan recognized each other's sphere of influence by the Taft-Katsura agreement. This meant that the US approved of Japan's spheres of influence in Korea and Manchuria. Harriman's purchase of south Manchurian railways was opposed by Japan, which was determined to expand its sphere of influence in Manchuria. President Roosevelt resolved the domestic anti-Japanese sentiments by a gentlemen's agreement from 1907 to 1909. He balanced domestic politics with diplomacy. At the same time, he demonstrated that he was not afraid of Japan by dispatching the Great White Fleet, which consisted of sixteen war ships to Japan. The US maintained Chinese integrity by the Root-Takahira Agreement. President Roosevelt was trying to reduce Japanese immigration to the US and understood that the defense of the Philippines would be difficult in case of war with Japan. Therefore, he avoided confronting Japan in Manchuria.

After World War I, the US did not participate in the League of Nations, favoring instead isolationism from Europe, while she opted for co-action in the Far East. For example, the US opened the Washington Conference in 1921 and made the Nine-Power treaty to aggressively pursue the Open Door policy toward China. The US partially participated in League Of Nations (LON) activity by sending representatives to the investigation team for the Manchurian Incident, which stemmed from Japanese expansionism in China. The direct cause of American involvement in World War II was not the European War, but the outbreak of war in the Far East.

(c) New Isolationism

Robert Tucker argued in *A New Isolationism* that the common point between the Old and New Isolationism is the question of US influence abroad, that is, Europe in the Old, and the Third World in the New. Points of difference between the Old and New Isolationism are: first, German American's opposition to participation in a war disappeared; second, isolationism based on a sentimental exclusiveness also disappeared; third, economic interdependency has become much greater today than in the past; fourth, it is physically impossible to be isolated today because of nuclear weapons; fifth, the US has become too much of a superpower to abdicate its global responsibility; and finally, Old Isolationism meant to isolate America from Europe and actively engage with Asia, while New Isolationism means to remain engaged in Europe and isolated from Asia.

Robert Taft, a New Isolationist, believed that nobody becomes isolationist today. He stressed an effective security system by international organizations. Another New Isolationist, President Herbert Hoover, recognized the necessity to defend Great Britain, Japan, Taiwan, the Philippines and Australia, as well as New Zealand, if necessary. Fulbright, McGovern, Lippman and Kennan insisted on promoting the UN role, to maintain vital alliance relations with the US, and to negotiate with China and the Soviet Union. Even though Dean Acheson criticized George Kennan as being an isolationist, Kennan did not want to forego all 'entangling alliances' as the old isolationists did. However, he insisted on firm commitments to American vital interests.

In conclusion, New Isolationism is a quite different from Old Isolationism; therefore Old Isolationism would never be revitalized.

(d) Policy suitability today

The benefit of isolationism would be that the US does not need to deploy its troops outside of the homeland, so that its financial and manpower burdens will be lessened. However, in so doing, the US can neither effectively fight against global terrorism nor engage the rest of the world, and consequently, the stability in the region will depend on outside factors. Those ideas are represented by Chalmers Johnson's paper,[9] as provided by the CATO Institute[10] and the report of a study group of the Economic Strategy Institute[11] in the US. They are very good critiques but they do not provide realistic alternatives to maintaining stability in Asia without US military presence. Just during my three year Defense Attaché tour in Washington, DC, US forces in the region contributed significantly to regional stability in such areas as the Taiwan Strait crisis in 1996, Cambodian turmoil in 1997, deployments to the Persian Gulf by the USS *Independence* carrier battle group from

Yokosuka in January 1998, the USS *Belleau Wood* amphibious readiness group from Sasebo as well as the 31ˢᵗ Marine Expeditionary Unit (MEU) in Okinawa in November 1998, and the USS *Kitty Hawk* carrier battle group from Yokosuka in April 1999. Additionally, another of Okinawa's MEUs was dispatched for the Indonesian crisis in May 1998, and joint patrols by the US 7ᵗʰ Fleet combatants with the Korean Navy against North Korean infiltration operations in 1998. Therefore, the ideas represented by Johnson have shock value only – to follow them would be irresponsible.

Asia After the 'Miracle': Redefining US Economic and Security Priorities issued by the Economic Strategy Institute underestimated the threats which Japan faces. For example, the study group concluded that the Theater Missile Defense system is not necessary to deal with missile capabilities likely to be developed by an economically impoverished North Korea in the foreseeable future.[12] A few months after they published the book, North Korea launched its Taepo Dong I, which not only flew over Japan but it was also reported that its third stage reached near Alaska. The Institute also wrote that Pyongyang has fully honored its verification and other commitments under its 1994 nuclear freeze agreement with the US. Yet, it was soon revealed that North Korea was continuing to construct its secret underground nuclear facility. Their perspective for the future of China's military capability was equally one-sided. They stated that Chinese conventional military capabilities do not pose a threat to Japan and insisted that the US pull its military bases back. But, they do not discuss future potential Chinese military capabilities which are growing yearly.

Those opinions are also consistent with the policy of the so-called 'the economy as number one priority.' This trend is dangerous because it treats Japan as a competitor, or even an enemy, and not as an ally. It is important to realize that economic and military strength are completely different dimensions of national power. It is a positive sum game in the economic arena, whereas it is a zero sum game in the military arena. The Geo-Economic school of thought, which tends to think of the economic arena as a zero sum game, easily overlooks this point. In other words, the world's largest and second largest military powers cannot get along with each other, whereas the world's largest and second largest economic powers are able to maintain a genuine alliance. Japanese investment provides benefits for the US economy and conversely, Japan's financial difficulties after the late 1990s are a matter of strong concern by the US[13] Due to the economic difficulties Asian countries have faced since late 1997, the US government as well as the general public were concerned about Japan's fiscal health. The concern stems from the fact that the US market must absorb the Asian countries' exports if the Japanese economy were to have serious problems. Additionally, Japanese financial aid for South Korea, Indonesia, Thailand and the IMF would be a reliable contribution for the US. Economic activity is a cooperative operation from which both parties can benefit. If the entire Asian Pacific economy grows, the interdependence among each country, including the US will accelerate. It is also important to note that nearly every market is functioning under the security framework provided by the US military presence in Asia. Therefore, American military engagement in Asia is in America's best interests as well as Asia's.

2.   BILATERALISM

The US currently maintains several bilateral alliances with maritime nations in Asia such as Japan, Australia, and South Korea. There is another option, which is to ally with China, who will be the next potential great power in Asia. This option is very attractive for some US policy-makers, because the US National Intelligence Council (NIC) estimated in *Global Trends 2015* in December 2000:

> China has been riding the crest of significant wave of economic growth for two decades. Many experts assess that China can maintain a growth rate of 7 percent or more for many years . . . We do not rule out the introduction of enough political reform by 2015 to allow China to adapt to domestic pressure for change and to continue to grow economically.

They also stated:

> In the view of many experts, Japan will have difficulty maintaining its current position as the world's third largest economy

by 2015 . . . . The first uncertainty about Japan is whether it will carry out the structural reforms needed to resume robust economic growth and to slow its decline relative to the rest of East Asia, particularly China.[14]

Even though this analysis might be true, this economic analysis is based upon the GDP comparison by using purchasing-power parity data.[15] Based on this data, Chinese GDP should already be one and half times that of Japan, even in 2000. True GDP figures for 2001, however, indicate that China's GDP is merely one fourth that of Japan. Dr Thomas Rawski of the University of Pittsburgh estimates that China's economic growth in 2001 may have been between 3% and 4%, or about half of the official figure. He argues:

> In the three years between 1997 and 2000, for example, China's GDP officially grew by 24.7%. Yet energy consumption dropped by 12.8% in the same period. This cannot be adequately explained by more efficient energy consumption or the rapid growth of industries requiring less energy.

Dr Rawski notes that periods of rapid economic growth in other Asian countries, as well as China itself ten years ago, have coincided with increased energy use, high employment and rising consumer prices. Between 1997 and 2001, China's employment hardly grew at all, while prices fell more than 2%.[16]

Additionally, someone mentioned that the growth rate of the Chinese economy and lawyers in the US are the same, so that when Chinese economy becomes number one in the world, the number of lawyers in the US will be greater than the US population. People who believe this myth fail to perceive that linear growth does not necessarily occur. In the 1980s many Americans believed that the 21st century would be the Japanese era and many books such as *Japan as No.1* by Ezra F. Vogel sold in the US. However, no one says that today.

South East Asian countries' economies, which became a free market in the 1970s, had deteriorated due to the late 1990s currency devaluation. The Chinese economy started to bloom merely after the lift of economic sanctions for the Tiananmen incident in the early 1990s. The Chinese economy will face a great deal of adversity in the future, such as the enormous bad debt in national banks, unemployment problems, corruption of the social system, friction between the political and economic systems, the ethnic Chinese and a growing minority population, religious (for example, the Fa Lun Gong) problems, and important differences between urban (rich) and rural (poor) areas. Moreover, the future global power will be the country that leads the Information Age.

In this context, I find it hard to believe that China will be the largest economic power in the world. In 1905, one American magazine, *The Independent*, predicted that China would become 'the greatest military power in the world within the next quarter century.'[17] In 1908, Theodore Roosevelt portrayed China's wakening as one of the 'great events of our age.'[18] Roosevelt's characterization reflected widespread American optimism toward China, its future, and the future of American relations with China. But events did not develop as expected.[19] Even in the Ming and Qing dynasties, China never became an integrated state. And today, China has many integration problems such as Taiwan, Tibet, and western Moslem provinces, which will continue to be a source of turmoil in the future. Alberto R. Coll stated in his paper *Future US Naval Roles and Missions in the Pacific*:

> Internal contradictions of economic and social modernization in a society whose leaders refuse to allow the emergence of democratic political institutions might lead to the political and territorial fragmentation of the Middle Kingdom. In such a scenario, prosperous southern provinces might break away from the less successful northern and western parts of China. The security implications of this possibility are much less well understood than the challenges of China's emergence as a regional or even global power.[20]

Even if the Chinese economy becomes the largest in the world, the US will not share political values with China. Additionally, there are major obstacles between the US and China, the so-called 'five Ts' which are: Trade, meaning huge trade deficits (greater than that of Japan); Technology transfer of weapons of mass destruction including the satellite technology transfer disapproval by the US; and Taiwan, Tibet, and Tiananmen (human rights issues).

The key question is whether China can really be a substitute for Japan? In other words, will China accept the US bases in its territory and pay the Host Nation Support (HNS) costs, which Japan is currently providing? If the answer is no, who is going to provide American bases and HNS other than Japan? Even though China provides port visits for US Seventh Fleet combatants in Hong Kong, China has frequently cancelled these port visits on many occasions, such as after the American bombing on Chinese embassy in Beograd in 1999, the emergency landing of an American EP-3 on Hainan Island in 2001, and the American acceptance of the Taiwanese Defense Minister in 2002.

The April 2001 EP-3 incident indicated that China does not share a common standard with the international community. First, China insisted that no foreign country should conduct intelligence activities near the Chinese coast, even though a Chinese intelligence vessel crossed the Strait of Tsugaru three times without notification in May 2000 (even Soviet intelligence vessels never did such a blatantly imprudent activity during the Cold War era). Second, a much more maneuverable Chinese fighter hit a much slower US EP-3. And third, China clamed that the American EP-3 invaded Chinese territory, when the EP-3 made an emergency landing on Hainan Island. When North Korean exiles escaped into the Japan Consulate in Shenyang in May 2002, Beijing clamed that Chinese armed policemen entered the Japanese Consulate territory and arrested five persons because of concern for the security of the Japanese Consulate office. However, three of the five were female including a two-year-old girl and a pregnant woman. Chinese public claims are often incoherent and exaggerated for political reasons.

Since the beginning of 2004, Chinese maritime survey vessels have conducted many lack-of-prior-notification surveillance activities over the Japanese Exclusive Economic Zone (EEZ) surrounding Okinotorishima without the required official prior notification. Responding to Japanese complaints, China stated that Okinotorishima is a rock, therefore, Japanese EEZ surrounding Okinotorishima is not acknowledged. However, China has claimed many rocks as

Chinese territory such as the disputed Spratly islands. Two scholars in the Chinese National Maritime Bureau, Jia Yu and Li Mingjie published a paper, insisting on the above claim in May 2004.[21] The director of Chinese National Maritime Bureau, Wang Shu Guang also stated in July 2000: 'The ocean is a theater of international political struggle and the aim of Chinese maritime activity in the 21st century is strengthening the Navy and advancing the maritime interests.'[22] Should there be future conflict between the US and China over Taiwan, the eastern sea area of Taiwan would be the area of conflict. Okinotorishima's EEZ is on the sea rout from Guam to the potential conflict area. Interestingly, China's lack of prior notification surveillance started right after the US Department of Defense Quadrennial Defense Review (QDR) in 2001 which stressed the strategic importance of the Western Pacific.[23] Accordingly American vessels stationed or visiting Guam have increased, and Chinese surveillance activity in the Japanese EEZ surrounding Okinotorishima has expanded. That may not be in the best interest of the US.

John K. Fairbank stated in his book *The Chinese World Order*:

The relation of the Chinese with surrounding areas, and with non-Chinese peoples generally, were colored by this concept of Sinocentrism and an assumption of Chinese superiority. The Chinese tended to think of their foreign relations as giving expression externally to the same principles of social and political order that were manifested internally within the Chinese states and society. China's foreign relations were accordingly hierarchic and nonegalitarian, like Chinese society itself. In the course of time, there grew up a network of Sino-foreign relations that roughly corresponded in East Asia to the international order that grew up in Europe, although as we shall see international and even interstate do not seem appropriate terms for it. We prefer to call it the Chinese world order.[24]

Japan has been a Chinese neighbor for more than 2000 years and understands China intimately. China is naturally a self-centered country that believes the world revolves around it. No matter how much the US wants to make China a Westernized and democratic state, China will not follow the

US easily. In this sense, China will never be a strategic partner of the US.

Surprisingly, Nicholas John Spykman had considerable foresight in 1942 when he stated that:

> Japan can act a buffer and balance against continental threats to the United States and against American threats to the Asianic mainland. The United States can be effective on that mainland in a military sense only in alliance with Japanese sea power and not against it. As in Great Britain, Japan's sea power can become available as an instrument for distant operations only when the continent is balanced and Japan's insular security assured. Because Japan lies across our path and is the most important Asiatic sea power, it is her power politics more than that of any other state that has defined our relations to the Asiatic balance.[25]

3.   MULTILATERALISM

If a multilateral security relationship like NATO is created in Asia, the US burden would lessen. However, the feasibility is low, because of the diversity among Asian nations, and their historical animosity towards each other. If a multilateral framework in Asia were to be established, it would be based upon the strong bilateral alliance structure that exists today. In this sense, the alliances in Asia are the core around which multilateral institutions and dialogue may be built, forming concentric rings of security.[26]

Dennis C. Blair and John T. Hanley, Jr. argued in their article 'From Wheels to Webs: Reconstructing Asia-Pacific Security Arrangements':

> The prevalent way of thinking about international relations throughout the Asia-Pacific region is in balance-of-power terms. Leaders in China, India, Russia, and other states talk of a multi-polar world where major states are rivals, continually maneuvering to create balance. This is the world of Bismarck and nineteenth-century Europe. An alternative approach, offering the prospect of a brighter future in Asia and better suited to the concerns of the twenty-first century, is one in which states co-operate in areas of shared interest such as peaceful development, diplomacy promotion, and use of negotiation to resolve

disagreements. In essence, it would be perfect to promote 'security communities.' Karl Deutsch coined the term 'security community' in 1957 to mean a group of states whose members 'share dependable expectations of peaceful change' in their mutual relations and rule out the use of force as a means of resolving their differences.[27]

Their idea of security community, I believe, comes from the theory of *Constructivism*. However, while this idea may apply to the post-modern sphere in Western Europe and North America, it is premature for Asia because there are so many countries in the lower modern sphere, such as China, Russia, and North Korea, who consider international relations with a 19th Century balance of power outlook.

The recent US efforts for *mini*-lateral national approach is working, such as six party talks among the US, Japan, South Korea, China, Russia and North Korea regarding North Korean nuclear issues and the second track trilateral talks among the US, Japan and Russia. Therefore, bilateral or multilateral are not always mutually exclusive courses of action, but can co-exist and sometimes even complement each other.

The United States and Asia: Toward a New US Strategy and Force Posture, published by the Rand Corporation in May 2001, stated:

First, the United States should deepen as well as widen its bilateral security alliances to create a larger partnership. This multilateralization – which would be a complement to and not a substitute for existing bilateral alliances – should include the United States, Japan, South Korea, Australia, and perhaps Singapore, the Philippines, and Thailand.[28]

In Autumn 2000, Kurt M. Campbell argued in his paper 'Energizing the US–Japan Security Partnership:'

One of the most important developments of the past five years in the security realm has been the growth of security cooperation between the United States, Japan and South Korea. As a result, the two US bilateral security alliances have taken on some trilateral characteristics. The initial rationale for cooperation in the mid-1990s was the challenge posed by North Korea. In actuality, that cooperation has expanded into a broader regional security framework. It is time that security specialists in all three countries consider what steps might be possible to provide a more formal trilateral framework. Such an understanding could help reassure the three states as they confront the prospect of fundamental change in North Korea. The goal would be to create institutions and procedures that transcend the division of Korea.[29]

Eventually, the US, Japan, and ROK commenced the first trilateral talks (TCOG) in April 1999 and agreed to meet together four times each year.

As Deputy Secretary of Defense Paul Wolfowitz so aptly stated:

One hears the argument that those alliance relationships need to be replaced by some new multinational structure of collective security. One line of argument says that in the post-Cold War era we should do away with security relationships that divide countries of the region. Another says that the United States simply can't afford to continue shouldering this relationship role.

In fact, new multinational security arrangements have little chance of working unless they are built on the foundations of the strong alliance relationships constructed in an earlier period. To those who say the United States can't afford it anymore, I would say that the United States couldn't afford not to. In fact, because of the greatly reduced threats in both Europe and Asia, the United States is able to sustain credible military commitments at greatly reduced costs, including overall personnel reductions of more than 500,000 and real expenditure reductions of nearly 50 percent, with the US defense burden down to about 3 percent of GNP, less than half of the Cold War level.

There are important ways, however, in which these Cold War structures can be complemented by new ones that bring together countries that did not have the experience of cooperating with one another or which may even have been adversaries. One of these is the ASEAN Regional Forum (ARF), which brings the ASEAN countries together with all of the major powers in the Asia Pacific region in a forum where it is possible to discuss common problems.

However, while ARF is a useful forum for discussion, it may be too large for actually resolving issues. For that purpose, one potentially useful mechanism would be the greater use of trilateral mechanisms which would allow parties to discuss problems of serious common concern in an environment in which their bilateral disputes are muted. For example, the United States, Japan and Russia could work together on common concerns about security in the Northwest Pacific; or China, Japan, and the United States might develop an agenda of common security problems to work on. While the United States would fit logically into a great many such groupings, there is no reason why it would have to be in all of them. In fact, an overlapping network of such arrangements might help to prevent any clear fault line from dividing one group of countries from another.[30]

In conclusion, the best policy to encourage stability in Asia for the US is to maintain the bilateral alliances with maritime nations, which are Japan, Australia and South Korea, while engaging North Korea, China, and Russia and establishing a mini-lateral-security framework. This is important in a global sense, as well, because the US–Japan alliance works well with NATO, and Japanese forward bases contribute to security in a global manner. Economically, if Japanese policy accelerates Asia-Pacific economic development as well as interdependence among each country including the US, the US will perceive that its military engagement for the Asia-Pacific region must be a great benefit for Asia. Increased trade opportunities and American direct investment in Asia will, in fact, contribute to security. In other words, when the ROK, which is still in the modern sphere, joins with the post-modern sphere through economic prosperity, more interdependence and a more peaceful environment will ensue. If Russia, China and finally North Korea join the post-modern sphere in the medium and long term, Northeast Asian security will become much more stable.

NOTES

[1] *A National Security Strategy For A New Century,* The White House, December 1999, p. iii
[2] Richard J. Samuels and Christopher P. Twomey, *The Eagle Eyes the Pacific: American Foreign Policy Options in East Asia after the Cold War,* 1999, pp. 4–5
[3] Selig Adler, *The Uncertain Giant: 1921–1941,* 1965

4   Robert Davis Johnson, *The Peace Progressive and American Foreign Relations,* 1995
5   Melvyn P. Leffler, *Open Door Expansion, World Order, and Democratic Constrain*
6   Wayne Cole, *Roosevelt and the Isolationism, 1932–1945*
7   Manfred Jonas, *Isolationism in America, 1935–1941,* 1990 (Second edition)
8   Robert Tucker, *A New Isolationism: Threat or Promise?*
9   Chalmers Johnson, *The Pentagon's ossified strategy, East Asian Security,* Foreign Affairs, July 1995
10   Ted Galen Carpenter, *Paternalism and dependence,* Policy Analysis, November 1 1995,: Doug Bandow, *Okinawa: Liberating Washington's East Asian Military Colony,* The US–Japanese Relationship and Policy Analysis, September 1 1998
11   *Asia after the 'Miracle'; redefining US economic and security priorities,* Economic Strategy Institute, June 1998
12   Ibid. p. 71
13   Robert Rubin, Testimony before the House Banking Committee on the Global Economy, September 16, 1998, and Lawrence H. Summers, Testimony before the Senate Budget Committee, September 23, 1998
14   *Global Trends 2015,* US National Intelligence Council, December 2000
15   *GDP by Major Countries and EU: 2000 and 2015,* CIA's Long Term Growth Model
16   Thomas Rawski, 'How cooked are the books?', *The Economist,* March 16, 2002
17   'The Awakening of China', *The Independent* 57, April 20, 1905: 916
18   Theodore Roosevelt, *The Awakening China, Outlook* 90, November 28, 1908: 666
19   James Przystup, *China, Japan, and the United States,* the Council on Foreign Relations, 1999, p. 28
20   Alberto R. Coll, *Future US Naval Roles and Missions in the Pacific,* Naval War College, 2000, p. 7
21   Jia Yu and Li Mingjie, http://www.sina.com.cn, May 24, 2004
22   Wang Shu Guang, http://www. soa.gov.cn, July 2000
23   US Department of Defense, *Quadrennial Defense Review Report,* September 30, 2001, p. 27
24   John K. Fairbank, *The Chinese World Order,* Harvard East Asian Series 32, 1968, p. 2

25 Nicholas John Spykman, *America's Strategy in World Politics*, Institute of International Studies, Yale University, 1942, pp. 136–7

26 Joseph S. Nye, Jr., *The United States and East Asia: Working Together for a Secure Future*, July 1995

27 Dennis C. Blair and John T. Hanley Jr., 'From Wheels to Webs: Reconstructing Asia-Pacific Security Arrangements', *The Washington Quarterly*, Winter 2001

28 *The United States and Asia: Toward a New US Strategy and Force Posture*, Rand Corporation, May 2001, p. 47

29 Kurt M. Campbell, 'Energizing the US–Japan Security Partnership,' *The Washington Quarterly*, Autumn 2000, p. 130

30 Paul Wolfowitz, *Managing Our Way To A Peaceful Century*, The Trilateral Commission, July 1997, pp. 55–56

5

The US–Japan Alliance Rationale for Asian Countries

1. GENERAL TREND

Most Asian countries appreciate the US–Japan alliance for two primary reasons: first, the largest and second largest economic powers' friendly relationship creates tremendous stability in the Asian-Pacific region, and second, they think that the US–Japan alliance contains Japanese militarism or expansionism, even though the Japanese do not have such intentions. This is the so-called 'cork in the bottle'[1] theory. Robert E. Osgood also argued in his book *Alliances and American Foreign Policy*, 'There are four principal functions of alliances . . . the most prominent function of alliance has been to restrain and control allies, particularly in order to safeguard one ally against actions of another that might endanger its security or otherwise jeopardize its interests.'[2] Therefore, we cannot ignore the Asian perception.

2. STRATEGIC TRIANGLE BETWEEN THE US–JAPAN–CHINA

Recently, many people have come to believe that a strategic triangle made up of the US, Japan and China will be the key issue for the 21st century.[3] Physically, the triangle is strong, but geopolitically, it tends to have a two against one relationship. During World War II, the US. and China fought against Japan, and currently the US and Japan alliance leans against

China. The worst scenario for the US would be if China and Japan gang up against the US However, this scenario is unrealistic for several reasons. First, China and Japan neither share the same values nor do they trust each other. For example, it is not realistic for Japan to rely on the Chinese nuclear umbrella. Second, Japan as a maritime nation benefits little from allying with a land power, which could provide little contribution to protect our sea lines of communication. Third, breaking the alliance with the US is of absolutely no benefit to Japan at all.

Future potential conflicts in Asia may be caused by a Chinese energy shortage.[4] Since China became an oil importing country, it had to look for new oil supplies. The growing Chinese economy may use its accumulated financial resources to build up the People's Liberation Army (PLA) in order to take by force or intimidation potential oil resource in areas such as Senkaku, Spratly, and Paracel Islands, or interdict Japanese sea lines of communication to the Persian Gulf.

The best strategy to stabilize the triangular relationship among the US, Japan, and China is to push or pull China into the international community, with regulations and norms based on the close coordination between the US and Japan. Kurt M. Campbell argued in his paper *Energizing the US–Japan Security Partnership*:

> There has been remarkably little comparable dialogue among the three major powers of Asia: China, the United States, and Japan. It is certainly premature to consider any formal mechanism to accomplish this task, but there are a number of steps in the Track II and official dialogues that could be developed to improve trust and confidence on the margins. A series of complex negotiation is likely to be the root of any form of strategic reassurance among the three. The United States must convince China it does not seek to contain its rise, and it must persuade Japan that Washington will continue to be a reliable and steady partner. Japan must convince China that it will sincerely deal with the issue of history and persuade the United States that it will continue to support the burden of the US forward presence, both materially and politically. China must convince the United States that it sees Asia as big enough for both of them, now and in the future, and it must accept an increased Japanese role in the security affairs of Asia. It is hard

to imagine a continuing future of peace and stability in Asia unless these three powers can negotiate a kind of strategic *Modus Operandi*. Greater informal trilateral dialogue can also reduce Chinese uncertainties about the purposes behind the US–Japan political and security alliance.[5]

Dr Mike M. Mochizuki also wrote:

Greater US–Japan collaboration on economic issues concerning China, its accession to the WTO, for example, would reduce Beijing's ability to play Washington and Tokyo off of each other. Such coordination would also clarify to Beijing the acceptable terms of China's incorporation into the regional and global economic system. The smoother and quicker China's integration into international economic regimes, the more likely that a political elite will emerge in China that will be more cooperative on the security front.[6]

In order to do that, confidence building measures through defense exchange programs between China and Japan, as well as the US, will be a key issue.

3. CONFIDENCE BUILDING MEASURES THROUGH DEFENSE EXCHANGE PROGRAMS

Military people are usually considered the most conservative and the hardest liners because they kill each other during war. However, the reality is quite the opposite, especially after the Cold War. During and after the Cold War, military to military contacts have led to the formation of normal relationships among hostile or unfriendly countries. The US Navy had been in long contact with the Soviet Navy through annual meetings based on the Incidents at Sea (INCSEA) Agreement, even after President Reagan made the 'evil empire' speech in the 1980s. The military to military contact created further military cooperation such as exchange visits, joint exercises, and the joint patrols, which we see in Bosnia today.

The Defense Exchange Program between the US and China has been in progress since 1996. As part of those programs, Under Secretary of Defense (Policy) Slocombe and US Pacific Command Commander, Admiral Joseph Prueher visited

China in June and September, 1996, respectively. The Chinese Minister of Defense General Chi visited the US in December 1996. In March 1997, Chinese naval ships made the first ever port visit to the continental US. Each Armed Forces Chief of Defense – General Shalikashvili and General Fu – visited each other's country in May and August in 1997 respectively. Service Chiefs such as Army General Reimer (September 1997), Navy Admiral Johnson (October 1997), and Air Force General Ryan (May 1998) also visited China. Secretary of Defense Cohen made the first trip to China in January 1998. Finally, Chinese President Jiang Zemin visited the US in October to November 1997 and President Clinton visited China in June 1998. Even though Chairman of the Joint Chiefs, General Shelton, visited China in 2000, military exchanges between the US and China have cooled in 1999 and 2001 primarily as a result of the US suspicions regarding Chinese nuclear espionage, China's protest of the US bombing of the Chinese Embassy in Belgrade in 1999, and the US Navy EP-3 reconnaissance aircraft incident in 2001.

Japan has also continued Confidence Building Measures with surrounding countries after the Cold War, which are discussed below.

(a) Russia
The Japanese and Russian governments signed the INCSEA Agreement in October 1994. Japanese Minister of Defense Usui made the first ever visit to Russia (including the Soviet era), in April 1996. Russian Defense Minister Rodionov made the first visit to Japan in May 1997. In July 1996, a Japan Maritime Self-Defense Force ship made the first visit to Russia, at Vladivostok, since 1920, and a Russian warship visited Tokyo in June 1997, the first such visit in over a century. Former Japanese Prime Minister Hashimoto and Russian President Yeltsin met together at Krasnoyarsk in November1997 and agreed to expand the Japanese-Russian defense exchange program to enhance confidence building. Both leaders also discussed a joint maritime exercise in the Sea of Japan during the summer of 1998, and actually conducted combined Search and Rescue (SAR) exercises in July 1998 and September 1999. Then Japanese Chief of Maritime Staff, Admiral Fujita, made the first visit to Russia in February 2000. During the Japanese International Fleet Review

in October 2002, Russian Pacific Fleet sent a Slava class Guided Missile Cruiser and a Kilo class submarine to Tokyo Bay. Following Prime Minister Koizumi's visit to Russia in January 2003, Japanese Minister of Defense Ishiba visited Russia to discuss the development of a Dangerous Military Action Activities Agreement with Russian Defense Minister Ivanov. Ivanov also invited JMSDF to participate in a large-scale Pacific Fleet Exercise scheduled in summer 2003.

More than ten years ago, in late 1992, three Navy Captains from Russia, the US, and Japan, including myself, met at the Center for International Security and Arms Control at Stanford University. They produced a report entitled *Naval Cooperation in the Pacific: Looking to the Future*. As part of the proposals for Russia-Japan Relations in the report, they included the following future steps:

- Routine exchanges and ship visits
- Maritime cooperation
  - Humanitarian aims: natural disasters, at sea rescue, etc.
  - Counter-illegal activities: drug, piracy, terrorism, etc.
  - Joint exercises
  - Bilateral or multilateral cooperative security activities
  - Military VIP exchange
- Development of a Dangerous Military agreement.[7]

Both Russia and Japan have almost achieved all of these initiatives.

During the Cold War, Russia was a great potential enemy to Japan. Japan and Russia did not sign the Peace Treaty concluding World War II, because of the Northern Territory dispute issue. However, Japan hopes to provide a firm legal basis for mutual trust between the Japanese and Russian peoples by resolving the territorial issue and concluding a Peace Treaty, thereby dramatically improving relations between the two countries. The building of neighborly and friendly relations, and promoting cooperation without animosity between Japan and Russia would not only meet the interests of both countries, but would also contribute to lasting peace and stability in the Asia-Pacific region and the world. Therefore, the Peace Treaty settlement and building up of a friendly relationship with Russia will make a tremendous contribution to stabilizing the international environment in East Asia.

(b)   Korea

Though Korea has had a historical animosity against Japan, this has also been changing since the mid-1990s. In December 1994, the Korean Navy training squadron made its first visit to Japan since the end of World War II. The Japanese training squadron reciprocated by visiting Pusan in September 1996, which was followed by the Korean squadron's visit to Kure, the Japanese naval port in the Inland Sea in December 1996. Additionally, a Korean-Japanese military exchange student program to each nation's Service Staff College has been developing over many years. These exchange programs are a great contribution to the mutual understanding and confidence building between not only the militaries, but also to the countries as a whole – especially since Japan and Korea have harbored certain suspicions of each other for decades.

When South Korean President Kim Dae-jung visited Japan in October 1998, both the Japanese and South Korean governments agreed to end discussion of the so-called 'history problem' and to look forward to future bilateral relations. At that time, both governments also agreed to conduct a joint Search and Rescue (SAR) exercise the following year. Japanese Chief of Maritime Staff Admiral Yasumasa Yamamoto visited South Korea immediately after President Kim Dae-jung's visit to Japan. He agreed with his Korean counterpart to start the first Navy to Navy staff talks in February 1999 and to discuss a detailed schedule for the SAR exercise to be conducted the following August. This was a significant breakthrough for the collective defense right barrier, followed by the joint SAR exercise between Russia and Japan in July 1998. Because Japan Self-Defense Forces could not conduct exercises with foreign countries except the US Forces due to the collective defense right issue before that time.

In May 1999, Japan and Korea established 'hot line' communications between both Navy and Air Force headquarters. At the same time, two Air Force top-level meetings in Seoul were successful and a mutual exchange program for enhancing cooperation was announced. In 2000, Japanese Chairman of Joint Staff Council, General Fujinawa visited Korea in March and the Korean Minister of Defense visited Japan in May. Even though the defense exchange program between both countries was decelerated in 2001 due to the Japanese history textbook issue, the Korean Chairman of the Joint Chiefs of Staff, General Cho Young-kil, mentioned to me, as the President of the Japanese Joint Staff College in May 2001, that the ROK military was willing to conduct military exchanges even though they could not violate the principle of political control. Subsequent to our discussion, the ROK armed forces sent their first exchange student to the Japanese Joint Staff College in September 2001, despite Prime Minister Koizumi's visit to Yasukuni shrine in August that year.

The defense exchange program with Korea is in Japan's best interest because a total of two million troops with anti-Japanese sentiments would pose a direct and serious security concern for Japan should North and South Korea reunify.

(c)   China

Chinese and Japanese defense exchanges have been developing gradually. The Japanese Chairman of the Joint Staff Council visited China in February 1995, the first high military official's visit to Beijing after the Tiananmen incident. In August 1996, the Japanese Vice Minister of Defense visited China for the first time in eleven years. Then, Chinese and Japanese Defense Ministers visited Japan and China in February and May 1998, respectively. During the Japanese Defense Minister's visit, both Governments agreed to exchange top military leaders; however, the naval ship exchange program was not completely agreed upon. When Chinese Chief of General Staff General Fu Quan Yu visited Japan in April 2000, General Fujinawa, Japanese Chairman of Joint Staff Council, suggested future exchanges between naval vessels. However, General Fu's response was not enthusiastic, as far as I, as the Director J-4 in the Joint Staff Office, observed. General Fu mentioned: 'The military exchange program between Japan and China is important but Japan should not forget two issues. First; Japan should learn history. And second, the US–Japan Security Treaty should apply only in a bilateral context and not for the other country's sovereignty or domestic affairs.' In return, General Fujinawa visited China in June 2000. In November 2000, Deputy Chief of the General

Staff of the Chinese People's Liberation Army, General Xiong Guangkai visited Japan and talked with his counterpart, Administrative Vice Minister of the Defense Agency, Mr Ken Sato. Both parties agreed on a ship visit exchange. Chinese PLA ships would visit Japan in May 2002 and JMSDF ships will visit China in 2003. However, the defense exchange program between China and Japan was also decelerated because of the Japanese history textbook issue in 2001 and Japanese Prime Minister Koizumi's visit to Yasukuni Shrine in 2002. When I, as the President of the Japanese Joint Staff College, visited Beijing and talked with General Xiong Guangkai in June 2001, the general announced a clear intention to continue the military exchange program to me.

The military exchange program between China and Japan lags behind the other countries I mentioned above. I believe this is an area to be developed in the future because both countries' military personnel are suspicious of one another. If Chinese military personnel had the opportunity to meet young Japanese officers and talk to each other, they would see that Japanese military personnel have no aggressive intentions, and that the Self-Defense Force equipment is totally defensive in nature. Similarly, if Japanese military personnel visit Chinese military facilities, they may learn how defense expenditures happen. Transparency is critical to create mutual confidence-building measures.

As discussed above, my view is that the strategic triangle of US–Japan–China will be the key to future power balance in East Asia. Therefore, the defense exchange program and confidence building measures with the Chinese People's Liberation Army, which has strong political influence in China, will be one of Japan's key diplomatic issues. This will also contribute to the American engagement strategy with China indirectly.

(d)   Southeast Asia

Japan has been conducting politico-military talks as well as military to military talks with South East Asian countries since the late 1990s. Recent significant events include participation in multilateral military exercises. In October 2000, the Japan Maritime Self-Defense Force (JMSDF) participated in the Western Pacific Submarine Rescue Exercise in Singapore, in which the US, ROK, and Singapore also participated. Even though the Joint Staff Office and the services sent only observers, Japanese SDF personnel observed Exercise Team Challenge – a combination of Cobra Gold (Thailand, Singapore) and Tandem Thrust (Canada, Australia). This multinational joint exercise occurred in May 2001. The following month, the JMSDF again participated in the Western Pacific Minesweeping Exercise in which sixteen countries exercised together off the coast of Singapore. Finally, the JMSDF organized the Western Pacific Submarine Rescue Exercise in which US, Japanese, Australian, Singaporean, and ROK Navies participated (Chinese, Russian, Canadian, Indian and Royal Navies were observers) in the East China Sea from April to May 2002. These activities were also another breakthrough for breaking down barriers and building collective defense.

The waters of South East Asia are the key sea line of communication for Japan and South East Asia is also an important economic region for Japan. Therefore, it is important for Japan to promote security dialogue and mutual understanding in this region, especially cooperation against increasing piracy and maritime terrorism.

In conclusion, most Asian countries favor continuation of the US–Japan alliance because the alliance provides stability in the region, even though Japan needs a continuous development for the Confidence Building Measures with neighboring countries.

NOTES

1   Marine Corps Lieutenant General Henry C. Stackpole referred to this in his famous interview while commanding the III Marine Expeditionary Force in 1989
2   Robert E. Osgood, *Alliances and American Foreign Policy*, The Johns Hopkins Press, 1968, pp. 21–22
3   Susan C. Maybaumwisniewski and Mary A. Sommerville, *Blue Horizon: United States-Japan-PRC Tripartite Relations*, National Defense University, 1997
4   Kent E. Calder, *Pacific Defense*, William Morrow and Company, Inc., 1996

5   Kurt M. Campbell, 'Energizing the US–Japan Security Partnership,' *The Washington Quarterly*, Autumn 2000, p. 131

6   Mike M. Mochizuki, *Economics and Security: A Conceptual Framework*, The Council on Foreign Relations 1999, p. 245

7   Captain Moreland, Ota, Pan'kov, *Naval Cooperation in the Pacific: Looking to the Future*, Center for International Security and Arms Control in Stanford University, February 1993, p. 15

6

Current Issues

The three years – from May 1996 to June 1999 – of my Defense and Naval Attaché tour at the Embassy of Japan to Washington, DC, are characterized by three major issues. The first year was the Okinawa issue, the second year was the new Defense Guidelines, and the third year was Ballistic Missile Defense (BMD) issue.

As a result of the US marine rape incident in September 1995, the Special Action Committee on facilities and areas in Okinawa (SACO) was established in November 1995 and the final report was made to the Security Consultative Committee (SCC) in December 1996. I flew to Tokyo to attend the SCC with Secretary of Defense William Perry.

I returned to Tokyo in April 1997 with Secretary of Defense William Cohen where the US and the Japan Defense Summit discussed the Review of Guidelines for the Japan–US Defense Cooperation (Guidelines). The SCC acknowledged the Guidelines draft in September 1997 in New York.

At the SCC in September 1998, when I was again in attendance in New York, both the US and the Japanese sides emphasized the importance of BMD. The Ministers reviewed the progress of bilateral studies, and they agreed to proceed with further work in the direction of conducting cooperative research.

After I returned to Japan, I was assigned to the director of J-4 (Logistics), in the Joint Staff Office, where I worked on logistic support planning to US Forces in the area surrounding Japan based upon the New Guidelines. In the New Guidelines, there is the Bilateral Planning Committee (BPC), which consists of the Japanese Joint Staff Office and the staff of US Forces, Japan. Under the BPC, there are several panels such as intelligence, operations, and logistics. The logistics panel, of which I was responsible, is in my opinion the most important and difficult panel. This is because the intelligence between Japanese and American forces is already well established, and the Japan Self-Defense Forces cannot operate together with American forces without some exceptions like Search And Rescue (SAR) due to the New Guidelines legislation. US logistics and host nation support requirements during contingencies in the region could potentially be very high requiring many Japan government actors, not only on the military side but also on the part of many relevant Ministries and Agencies. For example, the use of civilian ports as well as airports and hospitals, must be resolved by close inter-agency coordination. By studying some of these current issues I hope to prove this book's theory that factors relating to stability, interdependence and globalism combine to maintain and strengthen the US–Japan alliance.

1.   OKINAWA

Okinawa is located in a very strategic position. When Commodore Mathew Perry visited Japan in 1853, he also stopped in Okinawa. During World War II, Okinawa was the site of one of the bloodiest battles of the entire war. Okinawa was not returned to Japan as a result of the Peace Treaty in 1951, and the US occupied it until May 1972. Today, Okinawa is still located in the center of three potential trouble spots: the Korean Peninsula, the Strait of Taiwan, and the South China Sea. After the September 11 terrorist attack, US Marines in Okinawa were dispatched to the Philippines in order to counter the Abu Sayyaf Group. The Philippines remain strategically important to the US even after the return of American bases there. Immediately after the Okinawa rape incident in September 1995, Secretary of Defense William Perry came to Japan and stated that the US bases in Okinawa are critical for the stability in the entire Asian region. For example, the US depended heavily on the bases in Okinawa during the North Korean crisis of 1994.

Both the US and the Japanese sides have quite a few politicians and scholars who insist the US should pull the Marines from Okinawa. For example, the Brookings Institute published *Toward A True Alliance: Restructuring US–Japan Security Relations* in 1997. In their book, Mike. M. Mochizuki and Michael O'Hanlon made policy recommendations in which the Marine Corps would leave Okinawa by 2003.[1] One of the reasons, which Michael O'Hanlon discussed, was that there are only three to four amphibious ships in Sasebo, which can load at most 2000 Marines. Therefore, the US Marines do not need the 20,000 troops in Okinawa and that 2000 Marines is not enough for combat operations in the Korean Peninsula.[2] In response, I would offer the following observations.

(a)   The Navy-Marine Corps team
The Navy-Marine Corps team has a unique capability, which is maritime maneuverability and flexibility. They can swing around from the western shore to the eastern shore of North Korea within a day. The Army and the Air Force are incapable of doing so, only a Navy-Marine team can demonstrate this capability. From the North Korean side, this capability must present a tremendous threat because they have to prepare their defense not only on the 38th parallel but also on their eastern and western coasts. The North Korean military plans are, because of uncertainty, very likely extremely complex and much more difficult to implement.

During the Korean War, the United Nations Forces led by General MacArthur made a remarkable amphibious landing operation on the western side of the peninsula at Inchon in September 1950 followed by another amphibious landing operation on the eastern side, Wonson, in October of the same year. History tells us how effective amphibious operations were on the Korean Peninsula.

According to the *Far Eastern Economic Review* (December 1998), US-South Korean strategy for a possible future Korean War indicated that one of three major attack methods would be a two-pronged assault by the US Marines, one from the west coast toward Nampo, and the other from the east coast toward Wonsan. The other two major attack methods are air and cruise missile attacks on North Korea's artillery corps and armoured thrusts across the Demilitarized Zone (DMZ) towards Pyongyang. The article stated:

> The war plan envisions the possibility of amphibious assaults by US Marines landing at the narrow waist of North Korea to cut the country in two. 'The entire resources of the US Marine Corps would flow here,' says a US official, referring to the Marine division on Okinawa, another in California and the third in North Carolina.[3]

In this sense, most troubling for North Korean military planners must be the Marine Corps in Okinawa. Why should we eliminate a valuable military option while North Korea remains a threat to the stability of the region? Additionally, the year 2003 is already passed, and peaceful unification of the Korean Peninsula is still years away.

In October 2002, North Korea acknowledged they were developing nuclear weapons despite the US–North Korea Framework Agreement of 1994. Then North Korea removed UN seals and tampered with surveillance equipment at frozen nuclear facilities in December 2002. Finally, Pyongyang announced its withdrawal from the nuclear Non-Proliferation Treaty (NPT) in January 2003. Therefore, closing Okinawa is a terrible policy recommendation and it would send the wrong signal to the rest of the world. We would be wise to remember that Secretary of State Dean Acheson's wrong signal in January 1950, in which the Korean Peninsula was not included in the US defense commitment, helped initiate the Korean War.

(b)   Marine Expeditionary Units

A Marine Expeditionary Unit (MEU) consists of about 2,000 soldiers with three to four amphibious ships. This is not only true for the 31st MEU in Okinawa, also for the 11th, 13th, and 15th MEU of the First Marine Expeditionary Force (MEF) at Camp Pendleton, California, and the 22nd, 24th, 26th MEU of the Second MEF at Camp Lejeune, North Carolina. A MEU is a kind of spearhead of an assault with about fifteen days of war sustainability. It is followed by a MEF Forward, with about 17,000 Marines and thirty days sustainability until the MEF itself, about 60,000 to 90,000 Marines with sixty days sustainability, arrives on the scene. In Northeast Asia, for example, the 31st MEU from Okinawa could establish a bridgehead, and then a MEF Forward would follow. A MEF Forward consists of the Marine Corps Units in Okinawa and Hawaii loaded by Maritime Prepositioning Squadron Three (MPSRON 3), which is a joint organization involving the US Navy, US Merchant Marine and US Air Force airlift. The Merchant Marine vessels in MPSRON 3 consist of Mobile Vessels stationed in Guam. Therefore, it takes about four days to sail to the Korean Peninsula. During MEF Forwards' sustaining period, about thirty days, the First MEF in Camp Pendleton will prepare and sail to Korea. Therefore, it is not correct to say that 20,000 Marines in Okinawa are useless because only three to four amphibious ships are available in Sasebo. We should also recall that only two Marine regiments conducted the Inchon amphibious first wave operation in the Korean War.

(c)   The need for the Marine Corps in Okinawa after reunification of Korea
Would we need the Marine Corps in Okinawa after the peaceful reunification of the Korean Peninsula? My answer is yes, we would still need them. From the Japanese perspective, Japan cannot possess a power projection capability due to the Japanese Constitution. Therefore, American power projection and Japanese defensive capabilities make for a complete deterrence force. If Japan wants to possess a power projection capability by herself, not only the Japanese people, but also most Asian neighbors, will not support it. From the US perspective, they still need to prepare for other potential trouble spots such as the Strait of Taiwan and the South China Sea.

After the reunification of the Korean Peninsula, the US Army in Korea will probably return to the US. If this happens, the forward deployed Navy-Marine Corps team will become more important than even during the Cold War era, because of the post-Cold War Navy-Marine Corps doctrine, *Forward . . . from the sea*[4]. The US Marines in Okinawa will potentially be the only American ground force element in Northeast Asia, so their role could be even more important than it is today.

Furthermore, the Marines in Okinawa act as a stabilization force for humanitarian relief, engagement exercises,
and Non-combatant Evacuation Operations (NEO). Even in
the 1990s, US Marines in Okinawa were dispatched to
Bangladesh for relief activity in 1992, to Cambodia during
the country's political turmoil in 1997, prepared for the
potential NEO for Indonesia in 1998, and conducted various
combined exercises with other nations including Russia.
Again, after the September 11 terrorist attack in 2001, a part
of the US Marines in Okinawa were dispatched to the
Philippines in order to counter the Abu Sayyaf Group (ASG).
Following the massive Tsunami in the Indian Ocean in
December 2004, Marine Corps Lieutenant General Robert R.
Blackman Jr. stationed in Okinawa took command of the
Joint Task Force 536 and deployed to Utapao, Thailand.
Those activities would be extremely difficult and time con-
suming if the Marines were in Hawaii or in the continental
United States.

For the above reasons, both Japan and the US need the
Marine Corps in Okinawa for the foreseeable future. Because
the US–Japan alliance is based on a 'contract' in which the
US will defend Japan and Japan will provide forward bases
for the US forces, the reduction of US bases in Japan may
mean the reduction of the US commitment to defend Japan.
It is also true that Okinawa is heavily burdened, with about
75% of all US exclusive use land in Japan located there.
However, as a result of the past efforts toward realignment
and consolidation, the number of US facilities and installa-
tions on Okinawa today stands at thirty-six, covering a total
area of about 233 square kilometers in January 2004, compared with eighty-three facilities and about 278 square kilometers in 1972, when Okinawa was returned to Japan.[5]
Further reduction of US bases in Okinawa may be possible
without any operational degradation of capability. Since
future war will rely more on technology, especially cyber and
information warfare, dependence on massive members of
ground troops will lessen. Therefore, the best solution to the
Okinawan problem for the time being is the good neighbor
policy which the US has been conducting and effecting since
the rape incident, and rearranging base facilities without

any reduction of present capability, including the integration of US bases with JSDF and local civilian facilities. Eventually, the land occupied by facilities to be returned under the SACO final report (December 1996) accounts for approximately 21 percent (50 square kilometers) of the USFJ facilities and area in Okinawa, and outpaces the approximately 43 square kilometers of land returned from the time of Okinawa's reversion to the publication of the final report.[6]

Another method to reduce the burden for the people in Okinawa would be by transferring the training functions to other Asian areas. Kurt M. Campbell argued in *The Washington Quarterly*, Autumn 2000:

> The United States must begin to undertake a 'ground pivot' away from its near-total reliance on northeast Asian bases to a strategy that seeks a variety of operational arrangements and training regimes throughout Asia, including Southeast Asia and Australia. These arrangements range from completing new military facilities in Singapore, seeking new training opportunities in the Philippines and Thailand, and possibly deepening alliance ties in Australia with a permanent presence on the ground.[7]

Even though I believe I am correct for the most part, I take issue against the last proposal for two reasons. First, Australian bases are too far away, probably more than one week, to react to any contingency on the Korean Peninsula although this arrangement might please the North Korean military planner. Second, the Marine Corps is a package with amphibious vessels and minesweepers stationed in Sasebo now. Additionally, that package includes Marine aviation, stationed in Iwakuni. Furthermore, that Amphibious Readiness Group is a package with the Carrier Battle Group, which provides escort and striking capabilities, stationed in Yokosuka and Atsugi. If the US Marines in Okinawa were transferred to Australia, the entire Seventh Fleet also has to move to Australia. Is that possible? I think not.

2.   NEW DEFENSE GUIDELINES

The new Defense Guidelines were authorized on September 23, 1997 when the Security Consultative Committee, the so-called two-plus-two consisting of the US Secretaries of State and Defense, and the Japanese Ministers of Foreign Affairs and Defense, was held in New York. The legislation was passed in the Japanese Diet on April 28, 1999. I shall analyze the Guidelines review for cause and effect through three lenses – Japan, US, and surrounding countries, especially China. The new legislation has provided increased stability for North East Asia with the strengthening of the security relationship between Japan and South Korea. We can see North Korea's changing attitude through Dr Perry's diplomatic efforts, such as holding off its ballistic missile launch test as well as opening dialogue with the ROK and Japan. Additionally, the New Defense Guidelines provide Japanese logistic support, including civilian ports, airports, and hospitals, to US armed forces during Situations In Areas Surrounding Japan (SIASJ). On the other hand, the US military might provide a NEO capability to Japan in the case of the Korean contingency, because the ROK government does not want to let Japanese SDF units land on Korean soil. This is another example of interdependence.

(a)   Japan
There were three overarching reasons for developing the Guidelines in 1998: two of them were the Gulf War in 1990 and the Korean Crisis during 1993–1994. In the First Gulf War, Japan contributed only financial resources, except for some mine-sweeping operations after the war. Even though the financial contribution was almost 13 billion dollars, which meant every Japanese person from a newborn baby to the oldest senior citizen, paid about 100 dollars, the international community did not fully appreciate Japan's fiscal contributions. Even before the Gulf War, US naval combatants protected the sea lines of communication in the Persian Gulf during the Iran-Iraq war. Most of the oil tankers belonged to Japan, who provided little contribution to the SLOC effort. The Japanese people realized then that we should contribute to the international community with

perhaps more than just finances and even perhaps sometimes blood.

The Gulf War could be permitted because the Gulf is a rather remote area from Japan. But, if something should happened on the Korean Peninsula where the Japanese are next door and Japan did little to contribute while many American soldiers were killed, that could be the end of the alliance. In May 1993, North Korea conducted its No Dong missile-firing test. The US almost initiated economic sanctions against North Korea because of nuclear development suspicions. At that time the Japanese cabinet seriously discussed what Japan could do if the second Korean War had occurred. However, the Japanese government was not ready to cooperate with, and provide support to, the US in the event of renewed hostilities on the peninsula.

Laura Stone wrote:

> It is universally accepted in both Washington and Asia that Japanese cooperation will be vital to the success of the sanctions. North Korean permanent residents of Japan remit substantial funds to their homeland, and Japan has risen to become the North's third-largest trading partner. The degree of Japanese cooperation is a critical variable determining the overall loss of American lives if the long-standing Cold War on the peninsula suddenly turns hot. Much of American air, naval, and rapid-reaction support for its troops in South Korea is based in Japan. According to the Security Treaty, Tokyo's approval is necessary to send the Japan-based troops into combat. If that approval is not forthcoming, an American decision to proceed without it – in the event of a surprise attack, for example – would likely sound the death knell for the alliance as it now exists.'[8]

Based on the above two lessons learned, the Japanese government recognized that an ally should contribute not only financial resources, but also share the risk. Additionally, it was time to review the old guidelines because the National Defense Program Outline was formulated in November 1995.

Third, it was time to review the old guidelines because the updated National Defense Program Outline was formulated in November1995.

The effect of the new defense guidelines for Japan is first, to develop the software (management tools) necessary to conduct effective military operations and second, to expand Japan's security role in Asia. The Japan Self-Defense Forces have been building up hardware – tanks, destroyers and fighters – to a certain level. However, we are far behind in software, which means how to use those forces in an effective manner. For example, the Japanese government's crisis management capability is very poor, including trans- ministry/agency coordination and the national security structure. We have many legal restrictions on the use of the electronic spectrum for military purposes; we do not have any wartime Rules Of Engagement (ROE) and Japan Self-Defense Forces cannot effectively exercise joint operations. Regarding this last point, the new guidelines provided for operational functionality, such as search and rescue or Non-combatant Evacuation Operations (NEO), whereas the old guidelines categorized each service such as ground, maritime, and air. Geographically, the new guidelines' focus is on the area surrounding Japan. In other words, it stresses Article 6 of the Security Treaty, whereas the old guidelines mainly stressed Article 5, which refers to Japan homeland defense. In summary, the new defense guidelines are not an end state, but rather a starting point to formulate a US–Japan combined operational plan.

(b)   US
The US motivation to review the old guidelines was also based on two reasons. After the Cold War, the Japanese Special Advisory Group on Defense Issues published the Higuchi Report on August 12, 1994, entitled *The Modality of the Security and Defense Capability of Japan*. In this publication, multinational security frameworks such as the United Nations were put ahead of the bilateral security relationship between the US and Japan.[9] Many US scholars who read this report were upset, because they thought that it meant that Japan would join the multilateral security framework rather than maintaining the bilateral security relationship with the US[10] This caused anxiety for those American scholars who wanted to maintain the US – Japan alliance even after the Cold War.[11] This is one of the reasons behind Assistant Secretary

of Defense Joseph Nye's decision to publish *United States Security Strategy for the East Asia-Pacific Region*, the so-called Nye-report in 1995. This initiative resulted in the Joint Security Declaration between President Clinton and Prime Minister Hashimoto in April 1996.

The second incentive was the unfortunate incident in Okinawa in September 1995. American security officials were concerned that the US–Japan alliance would face a crisis moment. They thought that the alliance needed a strong bond and reviewing the guidelines was a suitable method.

The benefits for the US are, first, to reduce the burden during any crisis in East Asia and, second, to make Japan a more normal alliance partner. I would say that what the US really wants of Japan is to use civilian facilities such as ports, airfields, and mine-sweeping capabilities during an emergency. Originally, the defense guidelines review did what normal alliance countries had done previously. In this context, there are still people in the US who are frustrated with the new defense guidelines because it does not break through the collective defense right, which is prohibited by the Japanese constitution. However, working-level officials such as Kurt M. Campbell, former Deputy Assistant Secretary of Defense (Asia & Pacific Affairs) and many other academics including Michael Green believe an incremental approach is best for the long term, which I also believe is a more realistic method. They thought that the Japanese coalition government could break apart if the US pushed Japan into changing its current interpretation of the Japanese Constitution.

(3)   Surrounding countries reaction
Although there were many negative opinions in the mass media of each of Japan's neighbors, at least the official statements of the surrounding countries regarding the new guidelines was generally positive, with the exception of China. The Korean official position was 'support with caution.' ASEAN countries and Australia had a very positive attitude. Even the Russian position was fundamentally positive. The Chinese officials usually state their opposition in this way: the new defense guidelines create most Asian countries' suspicion. However, in fact the only country who harbors suspicions is

China. China still looks at the US–Japan–China relationship as a zero-sum game.

In any case, we could not get full understanding from China regarding the new guidelines. Therefore we, especially the Japanese military, should develop the defense exchange program and try to obtain Chinese confidence. This is another starting point toward regional stability for the future.

3. ACQUISITION AND CROSS-SERVICING AGREEMENT (ACSA)

This agreement is designed to positively contribute to the smooth and effective operation of the Japan-US Security Treaty and the efforts for international peace made under the leadership of the United Nations. Its basic principle is that when either side requests the provision of supplies, the other side should provide such supplies or services, and this basic principle applies to bilateral exercises, UN peacekeeping operations, and international humanitarian relief operations. Goods and services to be provided under this agreement are food, water, billeting, transportation (including airlift), petroleum, oil, lubricants, clothing, communication, medical services, base support and maintenance, and airport and seaport services.

This agreement was signed by the representatives of the two countries in April 1996, approved by the Diet in June of the same year, and went into effect in October 1996. The proposed amendment to the agreement provided that if any party to the agreement requests the other party to provide goods or services that are necessary for actions taken in situations in the area surrounding Japan, the other party may provide such goods or services to the requesting party. The SDF will provide goods or services in compliance with the bill for ensuring security of situation in areas surrounding Japan and receive goods or services relation to such activities. Japan and the US signed the amended agreement and the Japanese government introduced it to the Diet in April 1998, and authorized it in May 1999.[12] Based on the amendment, as the director J-4 in the Joint Staff Office, I worked on the Implementing Agreement (IA) between General Fujinawa, then the Japanese Chairman of Joint Staff Office and Lieutenant General Hester, then the Commander of US Forces in Japan. General Hester was acting on behalf of Admiral Blair, then the Commander in Chief Pacific. Both leaders signed the IA on September 24, 1999. *A National Security Strategy for a New Century* published by the White House in December 1999 stated that:

> In April 1998, in order to support a revised ACSA which expands the provision of supplies and services to include the reciprocal provision of logistics support during situations surrounding Japan that have an important influence on Japan's peace and security.[13]

This is the perfect example how the alliances are glued together by interdependence. By this agreement, the US forces enjoy great access to Japanese resources during Situations In Area Surrounding Japan (SIASJ). Also, the agreement shows us how the US–Japanese alliance has strengthened incrementally. In April 1996, the agreement applies for only bilateral exercises, PKO activities and international humanitarian relief operations, while the amendment applies for situations in areas surrounding Japan. After the so-called anti-terrorism legislation passed the Diet in October 2001, the ACSA applied not only to SIASJ, but also to any area in the world except combatant zones. Furthermore, it expands to not only US Forces, but also to other nations' armed forces. Finally, the new Emergency Law passed the Diet in June 2003, the US Ambassador in Tokyo and Japanese Minister of Foreign Affairs signed the so-called wartime ACSA in February 2004. The bilateral ACSA Procedural Agreement (PA) was signed on July 15, 2004 and ratified by the Diet with an effective date of July 31, 2004. These developments continue and they serve to illustrate the strengthening of the US–Japan alliance in the area of bilateral military cooperation.

4.   BALLISTIC MISSILE DEFENSE

On August 31, 1998, North Korea launched a Taepo Dong 1, which they claimed was a satellite. North Korea demonstrated the capability to launch a missile, which can fly over Japan. The launch demonstrated that they have the capability to deliver a weapon payload against other countries at increasing ranges, about 4000 km, to include the capability of reaching US territory. Not only was this a longer range than we expected, but their missile technology was such that they were able to launch a multistage missile, which was also further advanced than estimated. This North Korean action fundamentally affects Japan's security, and presents a very serious situation of great concern. It is also an act that is deeply regrettable from the viewpoint of peace and security in North East Asia and only heightens concern about the proliferation of weapons of mass destruction. It was reported that a Middle East country's delegation was sent to observe the last missile launch in North Korea. If North Korea sells this missile technology, it will pose a serious threat for America's friends and allies in the Middle East region.

In May 1993, North Korea conducted a test firing of an earlier missile, the No Dong, with a maximum range estimated to be about 1300 km (although *Chosen-Noppo* reported in October 1998 that the missile reached the Pacific Ocean). Therefore, the No Dong missile can cover almost the entire Japanese territory. The Taepo Dong 1, whose maximum range is about 1500 km, can cover all of Japan, including Okinawa. Finally, the Taepo Dong 2 is believed to be able to reach US territory.

North Korea is believed to possess chemical and biological weapons. In addition to that, US Secretary of Defense Rumsfeld stated in November 2002, that North Korea is assessed to have a nuclear weapon or two.[14] Pyongyang has admitted to possessing nuclear weapons and continues to try and develop the delivery system. These chemical and nuclear weapons may be put into the warheads of the No Dong and Taepo Dong missiles. That is a tremendous threat to Japan.

Theoretically, Chinese ballistic missiles can also reach Japan. CSS-6s (DF-15), which were launched into waters near Taiwan in 1995 and 1996, only have a 600 km range, but the CSS-5 Mod 1(DF-21) and CSS-2 (DF-3) have ranges of 1800 km and 2800 km, respectively. According to a *Washington Times* article dated July 10, 1997, the liquid-fueled CSS-2s are being replaced by newer and more accurate solid-fueled CSS-5s, and two of those missile sites, exist in the northeast of China, at Tonghua Launch Complex and Dengshahe Field Garrison – well within range of Japan. According to the Chinese missile specialist at the Heritage Foundation, China is developing DF-21X or CSS-5 Mods 2 and 3, with ranges of 2850 km and 3000 km, respectively. The significant difference between the DF-21 and the DF-21X is accuracy, with the DF-21X estimated as 50 meters Circular Error Probable (CEP) compared with the DF-21's estimated 500 meters CEP.

The Ballistic Missile Defense co-research initiative between the US and Japan has several implications. Technologically, this is a good example of two-way cooperation. So far, Japan has been criticized as a security free-rider benefiting from one-way military technology transfers from the US. In the BMD cooperation case, however, Japan can contribute technologies associated with Infrared Red (IR) seekers, advanced kinetic warheads, lightweight nosecones, and second stage propulsion, as Fukushiro Nukaga, then the Director General of the Defense Agency, committed at the Defense Summit talks on September 21, 1998.

Militarily BMD operations will typify US–Japan combined operations, as well as joint operations among the three services. Imagine, a US surveillance satellite detects a ballistic missile launch and transfers the data to a Japanese AEGIS destroyer at sea, and then the ballistic missile is shot down by the ship's missiles or Air Self-Defense Force Patriot missiles if the AEGIS fails to shoot. These missile defense systems will protect not only Japanese citizens, but also American troops stationed in Japan. Additionally, the Japanese AEGIS destroyer is interoperable with the US. AEGIS cruisers and destroyers, which are stationed in Yokosuka naval base. This is a perfect example of interdependence as I discussed earlier.

BMD has one more strategic implication in a global sense. If the US and Japan succeed in BMD cooperation, this will deter global proliferation of weapons of mass destruction because the BMD system will counter the ballistic missile threat, so that rogue nations have less incentive to develop and possess those weapons. We can also see the BMD cooperation as a typical example of alliance globalism. The BMD cooperation between the US and Japan, the *Arrow* missile cooperation program between the US and Israel, and the Medium Extended Air Defense System

(MEADS) cooperation between the US, Germany, and Italy will help deter global proliferation of ballistic missiles and nuclear weapons.

During the Gulf War, Iraq fired many Scud missiles at Israel. At that time, Scud launch information was detected by the US Infrared Red (IR) satellite and transferred to the US Space Command in Colorado through an Australian communication relay site, and provided to Israel. If North Korea launched the No Dong or Taepo Dong missile, the US IR satellite will detect it and transfer that data to the US Space Command in Colorado, who will then disseminate it to Japan. The operation represents a complete global manner.

After the Joint Statement was issued at the Security Consultative Committee on September 20, 1998, Chinese reporter Mr Zhu strongly criticized the potential US–Japan cooperative research for TMD (Theater Missile Defense – Ballistic Missile Defense consisted of TMD and National Missile Defense, or NMD at that time). He said that TMD would destabilize regional security and accelerate a regional arms race. The Chinese Ambassador to Japan, Mr Jin, also made a speech in Tokyo on October 27, 1998, saying: 'We recommend Japanese reconsideration for TMD research and deployment because first, it will create an arms race in the East Asia, and second, it will cause an internal interference to China if the TMD covers Taiwan.' However, TMD is purely a defensive system, so Chinese criticism must mean that China does not want to lose its strategic leverage against Japan. This is because the only power of influence China can bring to bear on Japan is a threat by ballistic missiles with nuclear warheads without bringing up past historic issues and potential massive human refugees, whereas Japan has many powerful ways to influence China such as economic aid.

BMD is like a bulletproof vest, and nobody views a person who wears a bulletproof vest as a threat. Only a person who aims a pistol at the wearer of a bulletproof vest must be unhappy. Therefore, the strong Chinese criticism would seem to verify that Chinese ballistic missiles are aimed at Japan. Japanese people do not want to give economic aid or ODA to the person who points weapons at Japan. Chinese logic here is the same as that used by the former Soviet Union, which strongly criticized the American Strategic Defense Initiative

(SDI) in the early 1980s. Moreover, Moscow and Beijing signed a five-year space cooperation agreement in July 2001 pursuant to which China and Russia will establish a special department on joint development of a regional missile defense system.[15]

Except for China, there is little disagreement regarding US–Japan BMD cooperation. Some objection exists, however, in the US not only in the Government but also in think tanks. Major opposition opinions come from Japan, such as from politicians and from some of the newspapers. There are political obstacles, such as the Three Principles on Arms Export and Resolution Concerning the Fundamentals of Space Development and Exploitation by Japan adopted at the Plenary Session of the House of Representatives on May 9, 1969. On April 21, 1967, then Minister Eisaku Sato declared the three principles during a House of Representatives' Audit Committee meeting. The Principles provide that arms exports to the following countries shall not be permitted: (1) Communist block countries; (2) Countries to which the export of arms is prohibited under United Nations resolutions; and (3) Countries which are actually involved or likely to become involved in international conflicts.[16] The Resolution Concerning the Fundamentals of Space Development and Exploitation by Japan is as follows:

> The development and exploitation by Japan of objects to be projected into space above the Earth's atmosphere, and of the rockets by which they are launched shall be confined to peaceful purposes only and shall be carried out to contribute to the progress of science, the improvement of the nation's living standards, and the welfare of human society, along with the development of industrial technology and voluntary international collaboration and cooperation.[17]

The typical opposition opinion is seen in an *Asahi Shinbun* article dated September 19, 1998. The argument, however naïve is that:

(1) Ballistic Missiles with conventional warheads are not a serious threat because of their inaccuracy. For example, German V-2 missile averaged only 2.3 deaths and 5.3

casualties per missile (although accuracy has increased exponentially since World War II).

(2) North Korea does not have the capability to make a nuclear warhead for their ballistic missiles because they have not conducted a nuclear test. Chemical and biological warheads are not suitable for ballistic missile delivery.

(3) Ballistic Missile Defense is very difficult. The US sea-based BMD program was scheduled to be complete in the year 2009, but it has been delayed. If the Maritime Self-Defense Force were to introduce the BMD system, it might be after twenty years, when the present North Korea may disappear.

(4) Cost for BMD will be 1.3 to 2.3 trillion yen – impossible to fund – because the current Self Defense Force equipment cost is 900 billion yen per year.[18]

I must take issue with this opinion. First of all, the article criticizes the BMD program without providing any alternatives. The article seems to insist, 'let's expose Japanese citizens to ballistic missile strikes.' Second, the article mentions only the North Korean missile threat (and dismisses any future North Korean potential nuclear warhead capability) but does not discuss the Chinese missile threat (with its known nuclear capability). Even if North Korea disappears within twenty years, how can Japan defend against the Chinese ballistic missile threat? Third, it is simply not true that it will take about twenty years for the Maritime Self-Defense Force to deploy the sea-based BMD system. People believe that deploying a functioning BMD system must be very difficult because the US Army's Theater High Altitude Area Defense (THAAD) missile had failed six times in a row by March 1999. However, THAAD finally succeeded in June and August 1999. Sea-based Missile Defense had four successes from 2002 to 2003. Patriot 3 missiles succeeded more than ten times from 1997 to 2002. The Israeli Arrow missile system also demonstrated successful Upper Tier capability in August 1996 and March 1997 and the Israeli Defense Ministry announced the deployment of this system in November 1998. And finally, former National Missile Defense, a much higher velocity test, was successfully tested in October 1999, July and December 2001, March and October 2002.

In 2007, the next of five Japanese AEGIS destroyers will be commissioned. Additionally, *Asahi Shinbun's* estimation of cost is somewhat exaggerated. Since we are going to use existing systems such as AEGIS destroyers, Patriot missiles, and probably AWACS, the cost would be only for modification and some new Command, Control, Communication, Computer and Intelligence (C4I) system devices (as well as any additional AEGIS destroyers). If we can introduce the Cooperative Engagement Concept (CEC), existing destroyers from the *Harusame* class, which has a vertical launch Mk 41 system, can be used in the same way as the AEGIS system. At the end of the day, however, even if *Asahi Shinbun's* estimation is true, we must defend our people and property against ballistic missile threats no matter how high the cost.

5.   INFORMATION GATHERING SATELLITE

After the North Korean Taepo Dong 1 launch, the Liberal Democratic Party (LDP) project team initiated the Information Gathering Satellite program. The Government of Japan committed itself to launching four information satellites by the Fiscal Year (FY) 2002 and requested the budget in FY 1999. Most Japanese and many Japanese newspapers thought that the US might object to a Japanese information satellite program, because the US would not want Japan to have an independent or strategic capability and because America would want to keep her information dominance. It was thought that this would be a source of conflict for the alliance. When the LDP project team and related Ministries and Agencies, representatives led by former Minister of Foreign Affairs, Mr Nakayama, and former Directors General of the Defense Agency, Messrs. Kawara, Tamazawa, and Aichi met Dr Kurt M. Campbell, the then Deputy Assistant Secretary of Defense (Asia & Pacific Affairs) on November 9, 1998 Dr Campbell conveyed a message from Secretary of Defense Cohen. First, the US would support and cooperate with the Japanese decision regarding the information satellite. Second, the US would provide technical expertise, training, and personnel exchange for the Japanese satellite program no matter whether the satellite was a domestic product or an import from the US; and third, the US would exchange information closely, including joint assessment for imagery interpretation. He also promised to cooperate and assist with regional coordination, to persuade China and South Korea that the Japanese satellite program meets a legitimate defense need. After several months of negotiations, US and Japanese governments signed a Memorandum of Agreement (MOA) in August 1999. *A National Security Strategy for a New Century*, published by the White House in December 1999, stated that our bilateral security cooperation has broadened as a result of research and development on theater missile defense and that America would cooperate on Japan's indigenous satellite program.[19] And the Institute for National Strategic Studies Special Report published in October 2000, stated: 'The United States should support Japan's reasonable desire to develop an independent intelligence capability, including its own satellites.'[20]

Therefore, the Japanese information satellite program is not a source of conflict but rather a source of cooperation. If both the US and Japan have information satellites and exchange the assessments, a better product will be created. It means that a competitive approach creates a better outcome rather than that provided by US information alone. This is another example of global and interdependent coordination.

This is a typical test case for the US–Japan alliance in the future. Though some in the US want to control Japan by the so-called 'cork in the bottle'[21] policy, Japan desires a more independent capability. Ultimately, this is an issue of trust between allies. If Japan initiated discussions to have strategic weapons such as aircraft carriers, the US would oppose it on the grounds that it can provide that capability, so that Japan would not have to spend huge amounts of money. If Japan went as far as to say that it wanted to have nuclear weapons, bombers, and a marine corps, the US would resist in the same way. However, the closest ally with the US, the United Kingdom, already has aircraft carriers, nuclear weapons, bombers and a marine corps. Therefore, these problems are really an issue of trust. Charles W. Kegley, Jr., and Gregory A. Raymond argued in their book, *When Trust Breaks Down:*

Alliance Norms and World Politics: 'Trusting states are able to rely on others, but mistrust states rely on themselves. In such an environment, alliances will be temporary, *ad hoc* arrangements, and alliance disintegration will be rapid and frequent.'[22] In the late 1990s of a booming American economy, the US Armed Forces were having a very difficult time maintaining human resources, because many people such as pilots, computer technicians, and doctors were going to the civilian sector where salaries were better than that in the military. In the US Navy, for example, each aircraft carrier battle group was facing a shortfall of about 500 people. Therefore, each person in the battle group had an increased workload and operational tempo became higher. This is why the USS *Independence* and *Kitty Hawk* carrier battle groups, who were and are respectively, stationed in Japan, were dispatched to the Gulf during the late 1990s. If Japan had possessed aircraft carriers during those periods, the US would not have had to worry about the unstable situation in East Asia, including the Korean Peninsula. US policy makers must consider whether Japan's security role should expand in the region and reexamine the 'cork in the bottle' theory.

In the early to mid-1980s, the Japan Defense Agency initially wanted to replace its F-1 support fighter with an indigenous aircraft based on both domestic and foreign systems. The US Department of Defense (DoD) insisted that cooperation take place under a government agreement with provisions for protection of information and technology flowback. DoD first raised the idea of co-development in late 1985. By early 1987, Washington had hardened its views on the use of an existing US airframe for Japan's Fighter Support Experimental (FSX) program. By late 1987, after a cabinet-level confrontation over 'US-based' versus 'indigenous' options for FSX, Tokyo had agreed to co-development based on the US F-16 fighter. This led to the FSX Development Memorandum of Understanding (MOU) the following year. Ironically, agreement on a joint FSX program triggered an even greater controversy. FSX had become a symbol for inflated Japanese expectations of aerospace leadership and fears for the US industrial base in Washington. In comparison with the FSX case, the information gathering satellite did not become a divisive political issue. Michael Chinworth analyzed why US concerns on this matter have subsided somewhat in recent years, and he provided the following reasons:[23]

- Few new, large-scale defense programs have begun between the United States and Japan since the FSX/F-2.
- US competitiveness is perceived as having rebounded.
- The Japanese bubble economy has burst.
- 'New Japans' such nations as the People's Republic of China have emerged in Asia.
- The US government now addresses the competitive implications of defense programs with Japan.
- The Department of Defense accepts the unity of economic and security polities.

There are clear distinctions between the FSX and the Information Gathering Satellite cases. During the FSX issue in the 1980s, the US was afraid of Japan's economic and technological growth because the Japanese growth rate was higher than that of the US. The US–Japan alliance is a unique alliance, with the winner and loser of World War II allied together. Therefore, the US does not want a Japan stronger than the US. This is the reason why Sparta attacked Athens. Thucydides says: 'What made war inevitable was the growth of Athenian power and fear which this caused in Sparta.'[24] The last *Soviet Military Power* booklet published by the US Department of Defense compared US and Japanese technological superiority. Most Americans in the late 1980s thought that the US was threatened more by the Japanese economy than by Soviet military power. Also, Washington thought that the FSX had an outstanding capability, while most of Japanese fighter technology come from the US. Today, however, the US has regained its confidence and it is not concerned about Japan's economy and technology because some American policy makers perceive that Japan has already passed her peak. Therefore, the US has not intervened in the Japanese indigenous post-P3C and Air Self-Defense Force transportation aircraft programs, so far. Finally, in November 2001, the US Government approved Japan's production of the sophisticated AEGIS system by four Japanese industries, Mitsubishi-Electronic, Mitsubishi-Heavy Industry, Oki, and NEC.

The United States and Japan: Advancing Toward a Mature Partnership, Institute for National Strategic Studies Special Report in October 2000, emphasized that they see the special relationship between the United States and Great Britain as a model for the alliance.[25] This means that the US must shift its policy toward Japan from that of the 'cork in the bottle' to that which holds Japan as a global and equal partner. To realize this, the US has to trust Japan in the same way that it does Great Britain, and Japan must, in turn, make further contributions for global security. The special report also devoted a large discussion to Intelligence and stated: 'The United States should support Japan's reasonable desire to develop an independent intelligence capacity, including its own satellites. Improving the quality of sharing requires immediate attention.'[26]

6.   THE US SECURITY STRATEGY FOR THE EAST ASIA PACIFIC REGION (EASR)

The first EASR was published in February 1995[27] and the second version was issued in November 1998. The first EASR was famous for the 'oxygen analogy:' you do not tend to notice it until you begin to lose it. The American security presence has helped provide this 'oxygen' for East Asian development.[28] This is another term for stability theory. The second version added several points to the first one such as the US Good Neighbors Policy, the recent development of US-Chinese military-to-military contact, and effective South Asian engagement including Singapore Changi Naval Station accessibility and the Visiting Forces Agreement with the Philippines.

The first EASR was called the 'Nye Initiative' because Dr Joseph Nye, then Assistant Secretary of Defense for International Affairs, developed it. At that time, the Japanese Director-General, Bureau of Defense Policy was Mr Masahiro Akiyama, who also made tremendous efforts on the report. The report is sometimes called the Nye-Akiyama Initiative. Three years after the first report was published, Mr Akiyama, who had become the Administrative Vice Minister of the Japan Defense Agency, and Dr Nye (who was then the Dean of Harvard's John F. Kennedy School of Government), met together and gave a seminar at Harvard University. I attended the seminar and pointed out to Dr Nye that the oxygen theory is no longer intact because oxygen is very passive, whereas US forces in East Asia in those three years were enormously active with such issues as the Strait of Taiwan crisis in March 1996, the Cambodian political crisis in July 1996, the USS *Independence* Battle Group deployment to the Persian Gulf in January 1998, and the Indonesian crisis in May 1998. American Forces are not 'passive oxygen,' but rather an 'active ambulance.' This means that the American Forces in East Asia have been making an enormous contribution for regional stabilization and the US military bases in Japan are essential for those activities. In other words, the US–Japan alliance is critically important for a stabilized Asia. Singapore Changi Naval Station accessibility and the Visiting Forces Agreement with the Philippines, as described in the second EASR, would also improve stability in East Asia due to important security issues in the region there, such as territorial dispute in the Paracels and Spratly Islands.

7. SEPTEMBER 11 TERRORISM ATTACK

On September 11, 2001, the post-Cold War sanctity of American life was shattered. At 8:45 a.m., American Airlines flight 11 slammed into the north tower of New York City's World Trade Center, igniting a massive explosion. As horrified New Yorkers and Americans across the country watched the blaze in person or on TV, United Airlines flight 175 struck the south tower some seventeen minutes later. American Airlines flight 77 plowed into the Pentagon outside Washington DC, slashing a hole in the building's side and forcing its evacuation. All that stood between another Washington landmark being struck and more innocent lives stolen was a group of passengers on United Airlines flight 93 who were not prepared to die without a struggle. Empowered by knowledge, a group on the plane apparently decided to attack their hijackers. Their plane crashed in rural Pennsylvania. No one on board survived. In the fall of 2001, military forces including aircraft, special operations forces, and naval assets from the United States and other nations began a protracted fight against a desperate but tenacious enemy in Afghanistan.

This time, the Japanese reaction was completely different from the one when the Gulf War started in 1991. The Japanese Government passed the special legislation against terrorism attacks within a month and dispatched several JMSDF ships to the Arabian Sea and JASDF aircraft for supporting missions. JGSDF soldiers started protecting US bases in Japan. These kinds of strengthening alliance actions had never happened since the US–Japan Alliance was established in 1952. *To Prevail – An American Strategy for the Campaign against Terrorism*, published by CSIS, stated:

> Japan in particular must play a visible role to avoid the damage caused to the alliance during the Persian Gulf War, when Japan's reluctance to assist the US – led coalition with anything but money raised serious concerns among the US policy elite and public alike about the relevance of the alliance to core US security interests. Japan's Prime Minister has led his legislature to make bold reforms in Japan's domestic law to allow for Japanese military support in intelligence sharing, mine clearing, refugee assistance, and other logistical and financial aid.[29]

President George W. Bush published *The Global War on Terrorism –The First 100 Days* and mentioned in it: 'The world has responded with an unprecedented coalition against international terrorism . . . Operation Enduring Freedom began on October 7, 2001, and enjoys the support of countries from the United Kingdom to Australia to Japan.'[30]

In May 2002, the US Department of Defense published *Coalition Contribution Fact Sheet* and stated about Japan:[31]

- Provide fleet refueling capability, placing two refueling/replenishment ships and three support/protection destroyers in the Area Of Responsibility (AOR). Through mid-May, this force has conducted seventy-five at-sea replenishments of coalition ships and provided 34.1 million gallons of F-76 fuel to US and UK vessels.
- Also as of mid-May, six C-130 aircraft had completed fifty-one missions consisting of 166 sorties with 773 tons of cargo and 123 passengers in support of re-supply and transport requirements within the Pacific Command (PACOM) AOR.

- On May 17, the Government of Japan approved a six-month extension of the Basic Plan authorizing the Self-Defense Forces to continue these efforts.

The Annual Report to the President and the Congress in 2002 stated in the section 'Strengthening Alliances and Partnership:'

> America's alliances and security relations give assurance to US allies and friends and pause to US foes. These relationships create a community of nations committed to common purposes. The defense strategy calls for efforts to strengthen America's alliances and partnerships and to develop new forms of security cooperation. The America commitment to these security arrangements bolsters the security of US allies and friends. Likewise, as witnessed in the wake of the event of September 11, NATO's invocation of Article V demonstrates the commitment of America's partners to collective defense, which bolsters the security of the United States.[32]

The National Security Strategy of the United States of America published in September 2002 stated: 'Japan and the Republic of Korea provided unprecedented levels of military logistical support within weeks of the terrorist attack.'[33]

NOTES

[1] Mike M. Mochizuki, *Toward A True Alliance*, Brookings Institution Press, 1997, Editor p. 195, 2.

[2] Ibid, pp. 145–146

[3] *Far Eastern Economic Review*, December 1998

[4] John H. Dalton, Secretary of the Navy, Admiral Jeremy M. Boorda, Chief of Naval Operations, General Carl E. Mundy, Jr., Commandant of the Marine Corps, *Forward . . . From the Sea*, Proceedings, December 1994, pp. 46–49

[5] *Defense of Japan 2004*, Defense Agency, p. 380

[6] *Defense of Japan 2000*, Defense Agency, p. 212

[7] Kurt M. Campbell, 'Energizing the US–Japan security Partnership,' *The Washington Quarterly*, Autumn 2000, p. 134

[8] Laura Stone, *Whither Trade and Security? A Historical Perspective*, The Council on Foreign Relations 1999, p. 247

9   *The Modality of the Security and Defense Capability of Japan;* Advisory Group on Defense Issues, 1994, pp. 11–17

10 For example, David L. 'Asher, A US–Japan Alliance for the New Century,' *Orbis*, 41, 3, Summer 1997, pp. 354–360

11 Funabashi Yoichi, *Doumei Hyouryu*, Iwanami Shoten, 1997, p. 259–264

12 *Defense of Japan 1999*, Defense Agency, pp. 234

13 *A National Security Strategy for a New Century*, the White House, December 1999, p. 35

14 DoD News Briefing, Secretary Rumsfeld and Gen. Myers, *News Transcript*, United States Department of Defense, Monday, November 4, 2002

15 *Annual Report on the Military Power of the People's Republic of China*, US Department of Defense, July 2002, p. 5

16 *Defense of Japan 1997*, Defense Agency, p. 342 Reference 36

17 *Defense of Japan 1986*, Defense Agency p. 294, reference 22

18 *Asahi Shinbun* article dated September 19, 1998

19 *A National Security Strategy for a New Century*, the White House, December 1999, p. 35

20 *United States and Japan: Advancing Toward a Mature Partnership (INSS Special Report)*, National Defense University, October 11 2000, p. 5

21 Marine Corps Lieutenant General Henry Stackpole referred to this in his famous interview while commanding the III Marine Expeditionary Force in 1989.

22 Charles W. Kegley, Jr., and Gregory A. Raymond, *When Trust Breaks Down: Alliance Norms and World Politics*, University of South Carolina Press, 1990, p. 256

23 Michael Chinworth, *The Technology Factor in US–Japan Security Relations*, The Council on Foreign Relations, 1999, pp. 290–291

24 Thucydides, *History of the Peloponnesian War*, Penguin Classics, 1954

25 Institute for National Strategic Studies National Defense Studies, *The United States and Japan: Advancing Toward a Mature Partnership*, October 2000, pp. 3–4

26 Ibid, pp. 4–5

27 *The US Security Strategy for the East Asia Pacific Region*, Office of International Security Affairs, Department of Defense, February 1995

28 Ibid, p. 1

29 *To Prevail – An American Strategy for the Campaign against Terrorism –*, CSIS, November 2001, p. 272

30 *The Global War on Terrorism – The First 100 Days*, The Coalition Information Centers, 2001, p. 3

31 United States Department of Defense, *Coalition Contribution Fact Sheet Update*, May 23, 2002, p. 6

32 United States Department of Defense, *The Annual Report to the President and the Congress*, August 15, 2002, pp. 20–21

33 *The National Security Strategy of the United States of America*, The White House, September 2002, p. 26

7

Future Case Studies

The following discussion examines whether or not the US–Japan alliance will endure in the case of future challenges. The first case study considers what happens if the Korean Peninsula unifies peacefully, the second case study covers the emergence of a democratic and market economy oriented China, and the third case covers a general trend of the US forward deployment bases. The first two of these are generally best-case scenarios compared to what could happen – a Korean War could start or China could become hegemonic state. Even in these best-case scenarios, the US–Japan alliance will endure. If the worst case were to happen, there is even more reason for this already strong alliance to become stronger.

1. PEACEFUL REUNIFICATION OF THE KOREAN PENINSULA

The US and Japanese national interests regarding Korean reunification are identical. Both countries want a peaceful resolution of the Korean conflict with a non-nuclear, democratic, reconciled, and ultimately reunified Korea.

At the end of October 1997, the Center for Naval Analyses (CNA) conducted its annual conference entitled *China, the United States, and Japan: Implications for Future US Security Strategy in East Asia*.[1] On the last day of the seminar, they ran a game simulation to explore the roles and basing of US military forces in East Asia after a hypothetical Korean reunification in 2002. Key players were former Secretary of Defense,

James Schlesinger acting as Secretary of Defense, former Assistant Secretary of State for East Asian and Pacific Affairs, Richard Solomon acting as Secretary of State, former Vice Chief of Naval Operations Admiral Stanley Arthur acting as Commander in Chief Pacific, former Commander in Chief of the United Nations and Combined Forces ROK/US Forces General Robert Sennewald playing his previous position, and former Ambassador to South Korea James Lilley acting in that position.

One player in the game, Chinese representative Dr Ding, mentioned that if Chinese relations with the United States and Japan were good, US forces in Korea and Japan would probably not pose a problem. The conference summary stated that the Japanese Prime Minister told the US President that Japan was deeply concerned over what a possible withdrawal of US forces from South Korea could mean. He expressed the hope that some US forces would remain in Korea to preserve regional stability in Northeast Asia. No participant insisted that the US–Japan alliance relation should be terminated.

Reality mirrors the simulation. Many Japanese scholars also participated, and on both the US and Japan sides, nobody wanted alliance termination. After reunification, the US–Japan alliance will increase in importance rather than be diminished, because of the potential for instability in a reunified Korea. There are many potential problems even if a peaceful reunification occurs. What kind of policy regime will be established? How does the reunified Korean government treat former North Korean leaders? Are there any possibilities for former North Korean security or military personnel to make a *coup d'état*? How do they get the financial aid to reconstruct the former North Korean region? How can they change the former North Korean social structure? What does the reunified Korean military organization look like? What about former North Korean nuclear weapons? It is not easy to settle down and it takes a long time to be stabilized. During the transition period, stabilization forces would be needed for a considerable period of time. This is the time when the US–Japan alliance will transit from the partial deterrent strategy toward North Korea to the complete stabilization strategy for the whole region.

2. DEMOCRATIC AND MARKET ORIENTED CHINA

Even if China becomes a market-oriented democracy, most Asian countries still do not want the US–Japan alliance to end, because it brings enormous stability to the Northeast Asian region. Japan's geopolitical situation and vulnerability will not be changed, which means Japan will still need American military power and its nuclear umbrella, unless Tokyo moves to acquire these capabilities. Yet even so, Japan will remain a vulnerable country due to globalization efforts. The US still needs forward bases in Japan for easy deployment from the Pacific to the Persian Gulf or Arabian Sea. The USS *Independence* and *Kitty Hawk* carrier battle groups stationed in Yokosuka deployed in January 1998, May 1999, October 2001, and February 2003 and the USS *Belleau Wood* amphibious readiness group stationed in Sasebo and the 31 Marine Expeditionary Unit in Okinawa deployed in November 1998 to the Gulf.

In conclusion, stability, interdependence and globalism theories are still valid and underscore the need for continuing the US–Japan alliance even if China becomes democratic with a market-oriented country.

3. GENERAL TREND OF THE US FORWARD DEPLOYMENT BASES

The *1998 Strategic Assessment: Engaging Power for Peace,* published by the Institute for National Strategic Studies, National Defense University, stated:

> If present trends, including a perception of a reduced threat from North Korea and recurring cycles of pan-Asianism, continue, the United States will face increasing pressure to reduce the size of its regional military deployments. This, in turn, may require considering measures to maintain presence while simultaneously reducing the number of forces, but it would not require reducing either the visibility of US forces or the ability of the United States to bring its power to bear. A key factor is building greater complementarity with military forces of the region.[2]

There are three major factors influencing the future of US overseas presence: (1) the changing security environment;

(2) the changing nature of warfare; and (3) the changing domestic factors. All of these factors interact with each other to affect the future of US forward deployed armed forces, their structures, and their capabilities. In particular, the changing security environment may directly affect the short-term perspective, and the changing nature of warfare, which is based on a Revolution in Military Affairs (RMA), may critically affect the mid- or long-term perspective. Domestic factors, including budget constraints and political realities, will continuously affect the future US overseas presence.[3]

At the end of the Cold War, many people believed that world peace would come and US forward deployed forces would not be needed. The reality, however, has been a different one. Former Chief of Staff, US Army, General Dennis J. Reimer, spoke in Washington, DC in October 1998, and stated that the US has engaged in thirty-two combat operations after the Cold War (1990), compared to only ten times during the Cold War era, from 1945 to 1989. In East Asia, there have been many more crises since 1990 than during the Cold War era, such as the North Korean crisis during 1993 to 1994, the Taiwan crisis in 1996, Cambodian political turmoil in 1997, the Indonesian crisis in 1998, and continuous North Korean infiltration, ballistic missile testing, and nuclear development. Therefore, the security environment has, in fact, worsened. The US forward deployed forces' operational tempo has been increasing and this trend will not dramatically change in the short term. Furthermore, the US President began the Global Posture Review (GPR) in November 2003. There are four overseas base categories: Power Projection Hub (PPH); Main Operating Base (MOB); Forward Operating Site (FOS); and Cooperative Security Location (CSL). The US bases in Japan are PPH, whereas US bases in Korea are between MOB and PPH or MOB category.[4]

In the mid or long term, however, the importance of US forward bases will decrease due to technological development and US domestic factors. For example, the US Air Force is developing the *Global Engagement* concept, which means some combat aircraft can take off from US territory and come back after the mission. *Global Engagement* states:

> Over time, technological change, threat to forward bases, asymmetric strategies by adversaries who seek to deny entry to US

power projection forces, and growing budgetary pressures will likely change the way the Air Force carries out its presence and power projection missions . . . The Air Force has relied heavily in the past on the elements of that mix that were permanently forward-based overseas. Currently, the Air Force is increasing the role of expeditionary forces to maintain its global engagement capability.[5]

Therefore, the significance of forward bases will not be as critical in the future. Forward deployed permanent US Army bases may also decrease significantly because of advanced airlift and sealift capabilities. The last remaining US forward bases in foreign countries might be Naval bases. This is another reason why the US–Japan alliance could become a 'Navy alliance.'

The important thing for Japan to notice, however, is that if the value of forward bases decreases, then the Japanese contribution to the US will be less important in the future. This is because the US–Japan alliance is based upon a give-and-take relationship, in which the US commits to defending Japan and Japan provides the forward bases and Host Nation Support. Therefore, Japan has to consider other ways to contribute to the alliance and that must include sweat and sometimes blood, sharing hardships like wartime host nation support, and sharing risks.

NOTES

[1] *China, the United States, and Japan: Implications for Future US Security Strategy in East Asia, 1997 Annual Conference Summary*, Center for Naval Analyses, 1997

[2] *1998 Strategic Assessment: Engaging Power for Peace*, Institute for National Strategic Studies, National Defense University, p. 48

[3] Col. Hironaka, JASDF, *The Implications of the Future US Overseas Presence in the Asia-Pacific Region*, 1996

[4] *Korean Donga*, May 19, 2004

[5] *Global Engagement: A Vision for the 21st Century Air Force*, Department Air Force, 1996, p. 11

8

Negative Factors for the Alliance

As Chapters 3 through 5 make clear, not only Japan and the US but also almost all other Asian countries support the US–Japan alliance. This suggests that the alliance will continue in the foreseeable future. Should the alliance break down, however, the reasons would be a mutual distrust due to an unequal contribution or an economic/financial dispute. When the burden of the alliance exceeds the benefit from the alliance, the burdened partner will leave easily. In order to maintain the sound security relationship between the US and Japan, both countries have to make an effort to sustain the alliance. Let us now address the potential factors that could cause the alliance to break down for both the US and Japan.

1.   THE US

(a)   Leaning toward China without Japanese consultation
In 1972, President Nixon visited China. At that time, the Japanese Government was informed of the decision with only very short notice. That kind of 'bypass diplomacy' created distrust in Japan and the distrust has remained in the Japanese psyche for a long time. Charles W. Kegley, Jr., and Gregory A. Raymond argued in their book, *When Trust Breaks Down: Alliance Norms and World Politics*, that in the spiral of distrust, the security dilemma facing the international community is created, not resolved.[1] Alliance partners always have security dilemmas of entrapment and abandonment.[2] After the Cold War, Japan is no longer afraid of being trapped into conflict

with the Soviet Union. Her concern today is abandonment by the US.

For example, former Ambassador in Tokyo, Walter F. Mondale, had noted that the United States takes no position on who owns disputed islands and has said American forces would not be compelled by the treaty to intervene in a dispute over them on September 16, 1996. Then, the US Department spokesman Nicholas Burns stated on October 3, 1996 that the US would take a neutral position on the Senkaku Island issue, which is a territorial dispute between Japan and China. However, the US and Japanese governments' official positions never changed: the US Government agreed that the US–Japan Security Treaty applied to Okinawa and other Ryukyu Islands including Senkaku since the Okinawa Restoration Treaty in 1971.[3] The US Navy even used Senkaku Island as a firing range during the US administration period on Okinawa. Therefore, there is no clear rationale for the US government to take a neutral position. In fact, when the US returned Okinawa to Japanese sovereignty in 1972, and included Senkaku Island under Japanese administration, China did not press the matter. The current US attitude toward Senkaku Island creates distrust in the Japanese people. Should armed conflict between Japan and China happen over Senkaku Island, Japan might be able to control the surrounding seas with the Self-Defense Forces. But what can Japan do if China responds by threatening Japan with nuclear weapons after Beijing loses face? These American attitudes may ignite a Japanese autonomous defense initiative including nuclear weapons.

From June to July in 1998, President Clinton made a nine-day trip to China – the longest by an American president to a single country since Woodrow Wilson's post-World War I sojourn in Paris. This trip was symbolic of an equally misguided 'China First' policy.[4] President Clinton did not stop in Japan on that occasion. Many Japanese suspected that the focus of US foreign policy for Asia might shift from Japan to China. In March 2000, President Clinton visited both Pakistan and India; however, he clearly showed that the US diplomatic axis had shifted from Pakistan to India. Alliances always fear both retrenchment and involvement. Since the end of the Cold War, the involvement fear has waned but the retrenchment fear still exists. American people should not forget the fact that US relations with China have generally been better when US relations with the rest of Asia, particularly with Japan, have been good.[5]

(b)   Ignoring base issue sensitivity
The rape incident in Okinawa in September 1995 caused a tremendous amount of work for both the US and Japan. After this incident, a US Marine F/A-18 dropped a bomb near Okinawa Island in December 1996. In September 1998, a drunken American Marine hit an Okinawan girl with his car and fled the scene; she died several days later. This accident negatively influenced the election for the Okinawan Governor in November 1998, although then Governor Ota, the anti-US base candidate, lost.

In January 1998, the USS *Independence* air wing conducted Night Landing Practice (NLP) in Atsugi, Iwakuni, and Yokota air bases with only one-day notification, though both the US and Japanese governments agreed on at least two weeks notification. The headquarters of US Forces in Japan explained that the reason for conducting this sudden NLP was urgent operational needs associated with the replacement of the USS *Nimitz* in the Persian Gulf. But the USS *Nimitz* had been stationed in the Gulf since mid-October 1997. The replacement problem did not happen suddenly. Those actions damaged the mutual trust which had been built up between the Japanese local population and US forces, and have had a negative impact on the reviewing process of the Defense Guidelines, as well as on the Futenma Marine Air base relocation problem (one of significant commitments of SACO).

(c)   Encourage pro-Constitutionalists
The US Department of Defense wanted Japan to provide a great deal of logistic support in order to conduct joint operations during the North East Asian crisis. Most of these desires were not met due to limitations of the Japanese Constitution. However, the US never will say that it wants Tokyo to revise the Japanese Constitution. For example, when the US and Japan began to revise the old 'Guidelines for US–Japan Defense Cooperation', the requirements were officially held to be within the Japanese Constitution.[6] The American position is probably due to two reasons. First, the US actually

drafted the Japanese Constitution during the Occupation period following World War II, and is, therefore, historically wedded to it. Second, the US does not want Japan as a strategically active player in North East Asia, the so-called 'cork in the bottle' theory.

Let us respond to these arguments. First, a half-century has already passed since the Japanese Constitution was established and the environment surrounding Japan today is completely different than that immediately after World War II. Second, Japan has consistently exhibited democratic principles since the end of World War II to the point that no Japanese wants either a return to a militarized society or hegemony in Asia. The above US movement has served to discourage people who want to revise the Constitution in order to effectively support US forces, as well as exercise collective defense rights during the crisis. In brief, my view would be: 'Do not throw cold water on those sound Japanese activities.'

2.   JAPAN

(a)   Inadequate contribution: prohibiting collective Defense rights and poor crisis management capability
The US–Japan Alliance would be severely damaged if major conflicts should happen near Japan such as on the Korean Peninsula and in the Strait of Taiwan and if, while US soldiers were spilling their blood, Japan was unable to make adequate contributions due to improper crisis management capabilities. Although Prime Minister Junichiro Koizumi swiftly established the so-called anti-terrorism legislation and dispatched several JMSDF combatants to Arabian Sea in fall 2001 (right after the September 11 terrorism attack), negative perceptions of Japan's willingness to support the US linger from the First Gulf War experience of both countries. The Japanese government contributed up to 13 billion dollars in the final stage of the First Gulf War but the process was incremental. It took almost one year to make the decision to send mine sweepers to the Persian Gulf. At that time, most US security specialists called Japan a 'reluctant ally.' It would be worse in the case of conflict in North East Asia, because this region is in Japan's backyard. What are the problems for effective

Japanese crisis management? Let us examine two categories, which are structural problems and legal problems.

i.   Structural problems

Based on the Cabinet Law (Article 4), which was established in 1947, the supreme decision-making authority in the executive branch is the Cabinet council and not the Prime Minister. According to custom, the Cabinet council vote must be unanimous. Therefore, a Cabinet council decision will not be made even if only one Minister opposes the issue.[7] However, in the case of a crisis and/or emergency, the Prime Minister should otherwise show strong leadership for the sake of national security. Otherwise, Japanese government officials cannot react in a timely manner.

The Cabinet Security Council, which was established in 1986, does not deal with huge refugee and great pollution incidents. The top uniformed officer, the Chairman of the Joint Staff Council, is not a permanent member of the Cabinet Security Council.

In the US, the Federal Emergency Management Agency coordinates with each Department and Agency during an emergency. Presidential Orders 10480 and 12742 specify roles and missions for each Department and Agency during a crisis, and the Defense Product Act establishes the mechanism for resource allocation and priority during wartime. However, the Japanese Government does not have such a mechanism for crises.

ii.   Legal problems

There are views that the biggest legal problem in Japan is the current official interpretation of the Japanese Constitution by the Japanese Government concerning the right of collective self-defense. That is:

> Under international law, it is understood that a state has the right of collective self-defense, that is the right to use force to stop armed attack on a foreign country with which it has close relation, even when the state itself is not under direct attack. It is beyond doubt that as a sovereign state, Japan has the right of collective self-defense under existing international law. The government, however, is of the view that the exercise of the right of

self-defense as permissible under Article 9 of the Constitution is authorized only when the act of self-defense is within the limit of the minimum necessity level for the defense of the nation. The government, therefore, believes that the exercise of the right of collective self-defense exceeds that limit and is constitutionally not permissible.[8]

This has constrained the Japanese contribution on various occasions such as the Gulf War and many peacekeeping operations and will be a strong obstacle if there is a conflict in North East Asia. Imagine: US Navy and JMSDF ships are patrolling together in the Sea of Japan during a future Korean crisis. If the US Naval combatant was attacked by a North Korean submarine and sunk, the JMSDF combatant would not be permitted to counter attack the North Korean submarine even though she may have contact on it. This is because Japan cannot exercise the collective defense right. The American public would be understandably upset and might demand that the US break off their alliance with such a country.

Through the new Guidelines discussion in the US, however, I found that there is a significant information gap between Japan and America. While the new Guidelines issue was the front-page headline on most Japanese newspapers in the late 1990s, the US newspapers did not treat the issue similarly. Therefore, while Japanese understand that we cannot exercise the collective defense right, most Americans (especially people outside the capital belt way) believe that Japan, who is a strong alliance partner of the US, must fight with American forces during any conflict situation in the area surrounding Japan. Should those Americans' expectations be betrayed, Japan would face a bitter reaction from the US.

The United States and Japan: Advancing Toward a Mature Partnership published by Institute for National Strategic Studies in October 2000 also stated: 'Japan's prohibition against collective self-defense is a constraint on alliance cooperation. Lifting this prohibition would allow for closer and more efficient security cooperation . . . Washington must make clear that it welcomes a Japan that is willing to make a greater contribution and to become a more equal alliance partner.'[9] I completely agree with this statement and believes that the prohibition against collective self-defense is absolutely out of date, because international affairs have became so global and current threats so transnational that national defense must also become transnational.

In 1998, Japanese and South Korean delegations conducted war games simulating Naval cooperation for a Korean crisis. During the simulation, South Korean representatives wanted combined operations with the JMSDF, while Japanese representatives were always saying: 'We cannot do that, because we cannot exercise the collective defense right.'[10] A future Korean crisis must be handled by the multinational framework we saw in the Gulf War, Kosovo, Afghanistan and Iraq, rather than just the US–Japan bilateral framework. This means that Australian or Canadian war ships, for example, must operate in the Sea of Japan. However, we cannot make any logistics plan to support them because of the collective defense right restriction. One of the great advancements after the September 11 terrorism attack on the US was that the Japanese Government created new legislation, which enables Japanese Self-Defense Force ships to provide logistics support for not only US Forces but also other nation's forces.

Retired Admiral Mutsuyoshi Gomi, former Commander in Chief, Self-Defense Fleet, researched many case studies about why Japan cannot employ its Self-Defense Forces during a possible Korean contingency. These are as follows:[11]

Case 1

The US Government consults with the Japanese Government and requests the launch of US military aircraft to attack the North Korean forces, and requests the deployment of US Forces to the Korean Peninsula from bases in Japan, based on Article VI of the Security Treaty.

Probable Japanese (GOJ) reaction: Although there were a lot of arguments regarding this prior consultation due to the great concern about the Japanese involvement of this conflict, finally, GOJ accepted the US Government request due to the Prime Minister's strong leadership that if Japan denies this request in this situation, it could mean the end of the alliance.

Case 2

Commander Seventh Fleet of US Navy (C7F) requested JMSDF cooperation to clear underwater floating mines seen to have been spread by North Korea from the high sea in the vicinity of the CVBG operational area. Such underwater floating mines are preventing the conduct of CVBG's smooth operation especially during combat operations against dark.

Probable Japanese Reaction: Japan states to C7F that JMSDF cannot cooperate because North Korean underwater floating mines are different from the so-called abandoned mines. JMSDF clearing of these mines operation before execution 'Defense of Japan' constitutes 'use of force' prohibited by the constitution.

Second, on the high seas in the vicinity of the CVBG operational area, there is a high possibility of existence of the North Korean submarines because a US Navy destroyer has already been damaged by an assumed North Korean submarine torpedo attack making this area regarded as the combat area. JMSDF minesweeping operations at this stage in this area are still controversial and may be prevented due to the interpretation that is integrating the SDF employment with the threat or use of forces by other country.

Case 3

C7F requests the JMSDF to conduct joint combined ASW surveillance operations more effective and smooth ASW operation.

Probable Japanese Reaction: JMSDF will conduct independent broad-area ASW surveillance operation outside of the combat area and provide the information to C7F. However, JMSDF cannot conduct joint combined ASW surveillance operations in the combat area with C7F due to the constitutional restrictions mentioned above. (After execution of Defense of Japan Operation, it is possible to conduct the coordinated ASW operation.)

Case 4

C7F requests the Japan Defense Agency to provide two ocean-going tugboats to tow the damaged supply ship from the sea off the Korean Peninsula to Sasebo.

Probable Japanese Reaction: Initially, GOJ intended to provide USN with JMSDF ships to tow the damaged vessel, however JMSDF has no appropriate towing ships also due to the constitutional limitation which prohibits from integrating the

SDF employment with the threat or use of force by other country. Therefore, JDA tried to charter a private company's big ocean-going tugboats within the condition from safety zone to Sasebo. However the labor union of that company strongly objected because the safety zone is very ambiguous, that is to say, difficult to distinguish between the combat area and safety zone because of North Korean submarine operations. So the Japan Defense Agency cannot help to meet C7F's request.

Case 5

The US destroyer escorting the US supply ship which had been damaged to Sasebo, was sunk on the high sea about thirty miles North from Iki Island. Whether by North Korean submarine torpedo attack or floating mines is not clear. Many crew members are floating on the dark winter sea and waiting rescue. C7F requests JDA dispatch SDF for rescue of this crew as soon as possible. Because of the present operational situation, CVBG's operating off Peninsula cannot afford to dispatch enough vessels and aircraft to rescue them.

Probable Japanese Reaction: According to the Law of situation in area surrounding Japan, 'Rear Area Search and Rescue Activities' can only be conducted outside of the combat area.[12] In this case, the possibility of North Korean submarines in this area is still high and floating mines are thought to exist. This area is apparently regarded as the combat area, so JDA cannot accept the C7F request.

Case 6

A CVBG operating in the Sea of Japan off the Peninsula to the East has conducted many air sorties to support ground battle in the vicinity of Seoul. Replenishment of ammunition, fuel, food, and weapons, etc. are required. Due to the retirement of the replenishment ship due to damage from the battle, C7F requested JDA to dispatch JMSDF supply ship to provide with weapons, ammunition, fuel and other items to the operating area and to conduct underway replenishment. Rendezvous point is to be determined.

Probable Japanese Reaction: JMSDF ships are prohibited from providing US Navy with JMSDF weapons and ammunition. However JMSDF ship can transport the USN weapons and ammunition. In this case, the rendezvous point should be outside the combat area and JMSDF can provide fuel and other supply items except for JMSDF ammunition and weapons.

Case 7

In South Korea, approximately 120,000 Japanese people remain. To conduct evacuation of these people, the Japanese Government had already dispatched a JMSDF transportation ship to the port in the vicinity of Seoul and is preparing to dispatch other ships. After the JMSDF transportation ship gets underway from the Korean port, JDA received information that the ship has a high possibility of encountering the North Korean missile boats attack. JDA tries to dispatch the escort ships. However dispatching the escort force to the combat area may increase the possibility of an encounter with the North Korean Naval ships and aircraft facing an engagement with them before they can rendezvous with JMSDF transportation ships. The execution order for the Defense of Japan has not been given by the government. This may lead to the potential use of force and possible integration of JDA forces with another country which the constitution prohibits. So JDA request C7F to escort this ship to the safety zone.

C7F answers JDA that US forces cannot afford to dispatch own escort force due to the present critical operational situation. These kinds of operations must be conducted under the responsibility of the respective governments.

Admiral Gomi concluded:

> The Japanese Government and people have to understand the vital importance of the Japan-US security relation for Japanese security and make much effort to show more positive combined cooperation and activities for the maintenance of this alliance. Also without the support of the US Government and people, this cannot be achieved. Of course, modifying the interpretation of the Japanese Constitution from prohibiting the collective self-defense to authorizing it is a Japanese domestic issue, however, at the same time, I believe it is an essential issue not only for Japan but also the United States national interest for the foreseeable future.

Japan's efforts to enhance world peace and stability began with the mine-sweeping operation after the Gulf War in 1991. JSDF also participated in Cambodia in 1992, Mozambique in 1993, Rwanda in 1994, and East Timor in 2002. Currently, the JSDF participates in the Golan Heights peacekeeping operations. From November to December 1998, JSDF dispatched its International Emergency Rescue Team for hurricane disaster relief in Honduras for the first time in its history. At that time, I received strong appreciation from the American people when I made a speech in Washington DC during my tour as the defense attaché.

In the National Defense Program Outline for FY 1996 and after, the Japan Defense Agency stressed the capability to respond to large-scale disasters and to contribute to the creation of a more stable security environment. However, the Japanese Government requires certain criteria to be met before Self Defense Forces are dispatched for UN Peace Keeping Operations. The basic guidelines for Japan's participation in peacekeeping operations, the so-called Five Principles, are as follows: First, agreement on a cease-fire shall have been reached among the parties to the conflict. Second, the parties to the conflict, including the territorial state(s), shall have given their consent to deployment of the peacekeeping force and Japan's participation in the force. Third, the peacekeeping force shall strictly maintain impartiality, not favoring any party to the conflict. Fourth, should any of the above guideline requirements cease to be satisfied, the Government of Japan may withdraw its contingent. Fifth, the use of weapons shall be limited to the minimum necessary to protect the personnel's lives, etc.[13] When the Japanese government examined whether the SDF should be dispatched to the East Timor PKO in September 1999, the Five Principles prohibited doing so. However, a Japanese contribution should be extended in the near future because the Japanese Government revised the Five Principles during the autumn Diet session in 2001. Due to the new revision, the Self-Defense Forces dispatched to the PKO mission will expand the subjects defended with the use of weapons and authorize the use of weapons to protect weapons and other equipment. Under the current political framework, it is impossible to send the Self-Defense Forces to a Gulf War-type conflict. However, the Japanese Government does consider dispatching

Maritime Self-Defense Force ships to the Maritime Interception Operation (MIO) against Iraqi smugglers in the Persian Gulf under the UN Security Council resolution. So far, Japanese Government has had resistance, not only on the domestic front, but also in our neighbors' reactions. China and the Republic of Korea would increase tensions if Japan stepped beyond the current interpretations of the Japanese Constitution. However, at least, the Republic of Korea has been shifting toward a more constructive manner so now is the time to change the Constitutional interpretations.

(b)   Anti-US bases campaign, especially in Okinawa
Even though a great majority of Japanese supports the US–Japan alliance,[14] the only internal problem in Japan is the base issue, especially in Okinawa. The Japanese Government relies on the Okinawa local referendum for public opinion regarding this important base issue. Because the referendum's questions are very simple (such as 'Do you want US bases in your town?'), the result of the referendum is always expected to be negative. Everybody in Japan, except a few communists and such, understands that the US–Japan security treaty is essential for Japan. But most Japanese people do not want to have US service members stationed in their town. Former Governor Ota in Okinawa used the negative results of the referendum as political leverage. Additionally, these anti-US-base campaigns would create negative public sentiment in the US such as: 'Why should we station US bases there when so many Japanese do not welcome them?' The US Secretary of Defense, Mr Rumsfeld stated at the Press Conference NATO Defense Ministerial on February 6, 2004: 'I don't want our forces in places that are inhospitable and where people don't want them there.'[15] Such a movement could have increasingly negative spiraling effects and might trigger a breaking off of the alliance. When the Japanese Government had a difficult time during the Nago city referendum regarding an offshore base facility to replace Marine Corps Air Station (MCAS) Futenma, the Japanese Government decided to set up a time limitation of 2015. But, this unilateral proposal increased the Pentagon's distrust a great deal.

History tells us about the case of Subic Naval and Clark Air Force Bases in the Philippines in the early 1990s. At the same time, interestingly, China promulgated its Territorial Water Act, which declared that all Paracel, Spratly and Senkaku Islands are in Chinese territorial waters. China has expanded her territory by taking advantage of a power vacuum three times in the past. First, immediately after the US withdrew from Vietnam in 1973, China invaded Paracel islands in 1974. Second, when the Soviet Naval combatants had decreased their activities near Cam Ranh Bay after 1984, China occupied the western part of Spratly islands from 1987 to 1988. And third, after the US closed their bases in the Philippines in 1992, China advanced her troops to the eastern part of Spratly islands in 1993.

Therefore, the people in Okinawa must realize that Okinawa is the engine room of the vessel named the US–Japan alliance. If the people in Okinawa want to stop the noise of this engine room by insisting on its removal, the US–Japan alliance vessel will stop and run aground. We have only to recall that the Philippine Government kicked the US from Subic Naval and Clark Air Force Bases in 1992, and tried to resolve by diplomatic means China's consolidation and expansion of their facilities on Mischief Reef in the Spratly Islands in 1998 – to no avail. Finally, the Philippine Minister of Defense visited the US in January 1999 and requested US support. However, the US reaction was very cool, because the American public did not want to help the country that kicked US bases out in the past. Consequently, the Philippine Congress ratified the US-Republic of Philippines Visiting Forces Agreement in May 1999 and established an ACSA in November 2002. Furthermore, President Gloria Arroyo said the US military had been training Philippine soldiers to defend the Spratly island against China until she asked them to shift the focus to fighting the Abu Sayyaf extremist group.[16] General Taiji Fujii, the former Japanese Defense Attaché to the Philippines from 1989 to 1992 said: 'The true reason that the US armed forces pulled out from the Philippines was that Filipinos robbed everything of value in American soldiers' housing after the American soldiers evacuated due to the eruption of the volcano Pinatubo. Most American soldiers thought they should never defend such a country.' We have to take this lesson to heart.

(c)   Security free rider
Usually, an alliance partner has to defend its partner when one is attacked. The US–Japan Security Treaty, however, defined only the US obligation to defend Japan. The Japanese contributions for the alliance are to provide bases in Japan and Host Nation Support – such as finance access rights or real estate. Though not only countries allied with the US contributed their troops for the many Gulf crises in the late 1990s, non-allied countries did so as well. Japan, however, the most important ally of the US, did not make any such contribution.

Moreover, the US transfers military technology to Japan, but Japanese dual-use technologies seldom go to the US. In this context, Japanese participation in the Ballistic Missile Defense (BMD) Cooperation Research Program with the US will be the great glue of the alliance in the early 21ˢᵗ century. Because the US would pull its military bases back to the American continent if Japan does not provide a ballistic missile defense umbrella. The BMD investment is not only for imminent threats including North Korean ballistic missiles, but also for countering global proliferation.

The Japanese Democratic Party's national security policy, 'no-bases alliance' as represented by former Prime Minister Morihiro Hosokawa's article 'Are US Troops in Japan Needed?'[17] is a typical example of the security free rider. This idea suggests that Japan will not provide the US any benefits during peace, but would ask the US to please defend us during war.

The US high officials are always saying that there is no bilateral relationship more important than the US–Japan one. If a Japanese believes that, however, he must be a very naïve person, indeed. The closest ally for America is the United Kingdom, because the UK always conducts military operations with the US, such as the Gulf, Balkans, Afghanistan and Iraq conflicts. Therefore, the US and UK are always sharing critical intelligence including offensive operations and the targets to be attacked. The next two most important allies for the US must be Canada and Australia, as there are many documents in the Pentagon which are classified as '*Releasable only to the US, UK, Canada, and Australia*'. When I, as the President of the Japanese Joint Staff College, visited the US Joint Staff College in Norfolk in June 2001, the Commandant mentioned that the senior course in there is opened only for US, UK, Australian, and Canadian students. Japanese students are not allowed to attend. Then, if someone wanted to know who the next two most important allies for the US besides the above three countries, the answer must be Germany and France. Japan is still not included in the Top 5. In autumn 1996, the US Department of Defense tried to construct a Command, Control, Communication, Computer, Intelligence, Reconnaissance, and Surveillance (C4ISR) architecture for coalition operations. The selected countries were the above five: UK, Australia, Canada, France and Germany. Japan was excluded. According to Kurt M. Campbell, then Deputy Assistant Secretary of Defense (Asia & Pacific Affairs), the two countries that the US is officially obligated to notify before any use of force are UK and Germany. Even in Asia, for example, Australian officers are invited as liaison officers in the Defense Intelligence Agency, while Japanese liaison officers are not invited. In conclusion, the US does not trust Japan as much as the above five states. The reason is obvious: Japan has not participated in the many coalition operations after the Cold War, including the Gulf War in 1991, another Gulf crisis in 1998, and Operation Joint Endeavor in the Balkans region in 1999. The US knows which countries have contributed their sweat and blood, and which countries have not contributed (or have contributed only money).

Bill Watts, who is the public affairs consultant for the Embassy of Japan in Washington, DC, reported in February 1999 that survey research indicated a slippage in Americans' view of Japan as a 'Close Ally/Friend.' According to the survey, the overall ranking of 10 countries on the basis of total 'close ally' and 'friend' scores is as follows:

1	Great Britain	88%
2	Canada	84%
3	France	46%
4	Germany	46%
5	Israel	46%
6	Japan	43%
7	Mexico	42%
8	Italy	38%
9	Poland	33%
10	Greece	32%

Though Watts missed surveying Australia, Australia must be ranked between Canada and France. Based on the results of the survey, we can understand why the US selected UK, Canada, Australia, France, and Germany as members of C4ISR architecture for coalition operations and not Japan. Even though Japan made a quick and supportive announcement regarding the US attack against Iraq in December 1998 (Operation Desert Fox) and France demonstrated a very negative attitude, France is a much closer ally with the US than Japan because France actually sent aircraft in support of Operation Northern Watch over Iraq – they, too shared sweat and blood with the US. Interestingly, Watts's survey indicated that percentages of 'Close Ally/Friend' for Japan has eroded in the past fifteen years. Numbers compared from June 1983 and July 1998 are as follows: Close Ally – from 16 to 8; Friend – from 45 to 35; Neutral – from 24 to 34; Unfriendly – from 5 to 11; Enemy – from 2 to 3; Not sure – from 8 to 9.

When the US–Japan alliance was established in 1952, the US GNP was more than ten times that of the Japanese one. Today, however, the US GNP is about two times the Japanese one, so that the burden and risk sharing should be adjusted according to Japanese economic power. Otherwise, the US burden exceeds its benefit and ultimately the alliance will collapse, especially if a crisis should occur.

NOTES

[1] Charles W. Kegley, Jr., and Gregory A. Raymond, *When Trust Breaks Down: Alliance Norms and World Politics,* University of South Carolina Press, 1990, p. 258

[2] Snyder, Glenn H. *The Security Dilemma in Alliance Politics* Vol. 36, July 1984

[3] Larry A. Niksch, *CRS Report for Congress 96-798F Senkaku Islands Dispute: The US Legal Relationship and Obligations,* 1996

[4] Robert Dujarric, *American Outlook Fall 1998,* Heritage Institute, p. 68

[5] Paul Wolfowitz, *Managing Our Way to a Peaceful Century,* The Trilateral Commission, July 1997, p. 57

[6] *The Guidelines for US–Japan Defense Cooperation* II. 2. 'Japan will conduct all its action within the limitations of the Constitution . . .', 1997

[7] Atsuyuki Sassa, *Politico-Military no susume,* Toshi Shuppan Kabushikigaisha, 1994, pp. 187–188

[8] *Defense of Japan 2001*, Defense Agency, p. 78

[9] *The United States and Japan: Advancing Toward a Mature Partnership,* Institute for National Strategic Studies, October 2000, p. 3

[10] Shinobu Miyaji, *This is Yomiuri, 1999.2,* pp. 274–282

[11] Admiral Mutsuyoshi Gomi(Ret.), *For the promotion of the Japan-US Security Relationship Aiming at the 21st Century,* Defense Research Center, 1999

[12] Rear area search and rescue operation
(1) Rear area search and rescue operation: Operation (Including transportation of those who have been rescued) Japan conducts within rear area to search or rescue combatants in distress due to combat activities (acts of killing and Injuring persons and destroying objects that are done as part of International armed conflict) that took place during situations In areas surrounding Japan.
(2) Rear area: Japanese territory and the high seas And the airspace above them in which no combat activities are taking place, and no combat activities are expected to take place for the duration of activities carried out within the area.

[13] *Defense of Japan 1998*, Defense Agency, p. 179

[14] *Defense of Japan* 1997 p. 219 Diagram5–5 Defense Structure

[15] *Secretary Rumsfeld Press Conference NATO Defense Ministerial,* United States Department of Defense News Transcript, Friday, February 6, 2004, p. 4

[16] *The Straits Times*, April 5, 2004

[17] Morihiro Hosokawa, Are US Troops in Japan Needed? Foreign Affairs, July/August 1998 Volume 77, Number 4, pp. 2–5

Conclusion

Alliances between developed states will endure due to the three factors of stability, interdependence, and globalism, even in the absence of any clear threat. However, history tells us that alliances break down when mutual distrust or an imbalanced contribution by either side exists.

It is desirable for not only the US and Japan, but also for most Asian countries, that the US–Japan alliance be maintained and strengthened. When the largest and second-largest economic powers ally together, global stability as a whole must surely be enhanced. Similarly, when the world's most powerful armed forces and one of the top armed forces in Asia, the Japan Self-Defense Force, work together, stability again must be enhanced.

However, as there are also weakening factors for any alliance, an alliance will continue only with the dedicated effort of both partners. The US–Japan alliance is a special alliance, as the obligation to defend the other partner is one-sided; in this case it is the obligation of the US and not Japan. Most US citizens, especially outside of the Washington, DC beltway, do not realize this fact, so the American people often react angrily when a crisis occurs in Asia and Japan makes little or no contribution. In order to avoid an alliance crisis, Japan should contribute not only as the forward military base provider or with Host Nation Support, but also with sweat and sometimes blood, sharing both hardship and risk. The new Defense Guidelines Review, amended ACSA, Ballistic Missile Defense co-research program, and recent contribution for both Operation Enduring Freedom and Iraqi Freedom are incremental approaches to increase Japan's contributory support of the alliance. However, this is not good enough. The Japanese government has to make a more focused effort, such as reviewing the collective defense right, which is prohibited by the current interpretation of the Constitution, and then take a more active role in stabilizing the region.

Because Japanese give in terms of the Alliance relation, the significance of providing forward bases will diminish due to a decrease in US forward deployment to Japan. During the Cold War, US bases in Japan were such a vital interest for the US strategically that it was reasonable for the US to have an asymmetric alliance, meaning that the US would defend Japan, but Japan did not have to reciprocate. However, regional conflicts in East Asia are not necessarily a direct security issue for the US after the Cold War. Now the issue is whether and to what extent this asymmetric alliance should be maintained. Furthermore, there are three reasons why US bases in Japan will diminish in the long term. First, the regional security environment: the Korean Peninsula will be unified sooner or later. Second, technological development: as we saw during the Kosovo and Afghanistan conflicts, B-2 bombers launched from the continental United States and dropped their bombs on Balkan and Afghan targets, then returned to their home bases. This means that forward bases will be not as critical in the future. And third, US domestic pressure especially from the Congress: overseas military personnel are becoming more unsafe because of the threat from international terrorism and Weapons of Mass Destruction (WMD). Therefore, Japan must provide more contributions than it is currently providing today to the US in order to maintain this vital alliance.

Bibliography

Adler, Selig, *The Uncertain Giant: 1921–1941*, 1965

Agreement between the Government of Australia and the Government of the Republic Indonesia on maintaining security, Jakarta, 18 December 1995

Agreement on Information Exchange and Establishment of Communication Procedures, Putrajaya Malaysia, May 7, 2002

Alberts, David S., Garstka, John J., Stein, Frederic P., *Network Centric Warfare-Developing and Leveraging Information Superiority-*, Department of Defense, August 1999

Alliance's Strategic Concept, approved by the Heads of State and Government participating in the meeting of North Atlantic Council in Washington DC on April 23 and 24, 1999

Ambrose, Stephen E. and Brinkley, Douglas G., *Rise to Globalism*, Penguin Books, 1997

Angell, Norman, *Great Illusion*, Garland Pub, 1912

Annual Report on the Military Power of the People's Republic of China, US Department of Defense, July 2002

Annual Report to the President and the Congress, US Department of Defense, August 15, 2002

Asher, David L., *A US–Japan Alliance for the New Century, Orbis*, 41, 3, summer 1997

Australia-United States: A Strategic partnership for the twenty-first Century, Jul. 1996

Australia-US Ministerial Consultation 1997: *Joint Communiqué*

Awakening of China, The Independent 57, 20 April 1905

Bandow, Doug, *Okinawa: Liberating Washington's East Asian Military Colony*, The US–Japanese Relationship and Policy Analysis, September 1, 1998

Bernstein, Richard and Munro, Ross, *The Coming Conflict with China*, New York: Knopf, 1997

Blair, Dennis C. and Hanley, John T. Jr., 'From Wheels to Webs: Reconstructing Asia-Pacific Security Arrangements', *The Washington Quarterly*, Winter 2001

Brzezinski, Zbigniew, *The Grand Chessboard*, The Perseus Books Group, 1998

Bush's speech in Norfolk, Virginia, December 7 during ceremonies aboard the U.S.S. *Enterprise* marking the 60th anniversary of the Japanese attack on Pearl Harbor, 2001

Calder, Kent E., *Pacific Defense*, William Morrow and Company, Inc., 1996

Campbell, Kurt M., 'Energizing the US–Japan Security Partnership,' *The Washington Quarterly*, Autumn 2000

Carpenter, Ted Galen, *Paternalism and dependence*, Policy Analysis, November 1, 1995

Challenges of the Global Century, Institute for National Strategic Studies National Defense University, June 2001

China's National Defense in 2000, The information office of the state council the People's Republic of China, October 2000

China's National Defense in 2004, The information office of the state council the People's Republic of China, December 2004

China, the United States, and Japan: Implications for Future US Security Strategy in East Asia, 1997 Annual Conference Summary, Center for Naval Analyses, 1997

Chinworth, Michael, *The Technology Factor in US–Japan Security Relations*, The Council on Foreign Relations, 1999

Clinton, 'Address to a Joint Sitting of the House of Parliament' *Current House Hansard*, 20 November 1996

Clubb, O. Edmund, *China & Russia*, Columbia University Press, 1971

Coalition Contribution Fact Sheet Update, United States Department of Defense, May 23, 2002

Cole, Wayne, *Roosevelt and the Isolationism, 1932–1945*

Coll, Alberto R., *Future US Naval Roles and Missions in the Pacific*, Naval War College, 2000

Cossa, Ralph A., *US-Korea-Japan Relations: Building Toward a 'Virtual Alliance'*, the Pacific Forum CSIS, December 3, 1999

Cronin, Patrick M. and Green, Michael J., *From Reaffirmation to Redefinition – An Agenda for the Future*, The council on Foreign Relations, 1999

Dalton, John H., Secretary of the Navy, Boorda, Admiral Jeremy M., Chief of Naval Operations, Mundy, General Carl E., Jr., Commandant of the Marine Corps, *Forward . . . From the Sea*, Proceedings, December 1994

Declaration of the Mexican/US alliance against drugs, Mexico City, May 6, 1997

Defeating Terrorism – New Strategy for the Campaign Against Terrorism, Center for Strategic & International Studies (CSIS) on November 27, 2001

Defense News, March 8, 1999

Defense of Japan, 1986, 1997, 1998, 2001, Defense Agency

Dillon, Dana R., *Piracy in Asia: A Growing Barrier to Maritime Trade*, Heritage Foundation, June 22, 2000

Dujarric, Robert, *American Outlook Fall 1998*, Heritage Institute

Economic Strategy Institute, *Asia after the 'Miracle'; redefining US economic and security priorities*, June 1998

Fairbank, John K., Reischauer, Edwin O., Craig, Albert M., *East Asia The Modern Transformation*, Houghton Mifflin Company, 1956

Fairbank, John K., *The Chinese World Order*, Harvard East Asian Series 32, 1968

Far Eastern Economic Review, December 1998

Fargo's speech at the biennial conference of the Asia-Pacific Center for Security Studies, July 2002

Freeman, Charles W., Jr., *The Diplomat's Dictionary*, Third printing, Washington, DC: United States Institute of Peace Press, 2001

Friedman, George and LeBard, Meredith, *The Coming War with Japan*, New York: St. Martins, 1991

Funabashi Yoichi, *Doumei Hyouryu*, Iwanami Shoten, 1997

Funabashi Yoichi, *Doumei no Hikaku Kenkyu*, Nihon Hyouronn Sha, March 2001

Garret, Banning and Glaser, Nonnie, 'China's Pragmatic Posture toward the Korean Peninsula', *Korean Journal of Defense Analysis*, vol. 9, no. 2, Winter 1997

GDP by Major Countries and EU: 2000 and 2015, CIA's long Term Growth Model

Giarra, Paul S., *US Bases in Japan: Historical Background and Innovative Approaches*, The Council on Foreign Relations, 1999

Global Engagement: A Vision for the 21st Century Air Force, Department Air Force, 1996

Global Trends 2015, US National Intelligence Council, December 2000

Global War on Terrorism – The First 100 Days, The Coalition Information Centers, 2001

Gomi Mutsuyoshi, *For the promotion of the Japan-US Security Relationship Aiming at the 21st Century*, Defense Research Center, 1999

Green, Michael J. and Cronin, Patrick M., *US–Japan Alliance: Past, Present, and Future*, 1999

Guidelines for US–Japan Defense Cooperation II, 1997

Harrison, Selig, *Japan's Nuclear Future: The Plutonium Debate and East Asian Security*, Carnegie Endowment for International Peace, 1996

Hironaka, Col., JASDF, *The Implications of the Future US Overseas Presence in the Asia-Pacific Region*, 1996

Holsti, K. J., *International Politics* Sixth Edition, University of British Columbia, 1992

Hosokawa Morihiro, *Are US Troops in Japan Needed?* Foreign Affairs, July/August 1998 Volume 77, Number 4

International Information Programs, US Department of State, Washington File, February 18, 2002

Ishikawa Toru, Address on the 50th anniversary of the Japan Maritime Self Defense Force at Yokosuka, April 26, 2002

Japan-US Joint Declaration on Security-Alliance for the 21st Century, April 17, 1996

Johnson, Chalmers, *The Pentagon's ossified strategy, East Asian Security*, Foreign Affairs, July 1995

Johnson, Robert Davis, *The Peace Progressive and American Foreign Relations*, 1995

Joint Staff Officer's Guide 2000, JFSC Pub 1

Jonas, Manfred, *Isolationism in America, 1935–1941*, 1990 (Second edition)

Kegley, Charles W., Jr., and Raymond, Gregory A., *When Trust Breaks Down: Alliance Norms and World Politics*, University of South Carolina Press, 1990

Keohane, Robert O. and Nye, Joseph S., *Power and Interdependence*, Longman, 2001

Kissinger, Henry A., 'A New National Partnership' speech by Secretary of State at Los Angeles, January 24, 1975 News Release, Department of States, Bureau of Public Affairs, Office of Media Service

Korean Donga, May 19, 2004

Krepinevich, Andrew F., *Transforming America's Alliances*, Center for Strategic and Budgetary Assessments, February 2000

LaFeber, Walter, *The Clash*, Norton and Company, 1997

Leffler, Melvyn P., *Open Door Expansion, World Order, and Democratic Constrain*

London Declaration on a transformed North Atlantic Alliance issued by the Heads of States and Government of the North Atlantic Council, London, 5–6 July 1990

Madrid Declaration on Euro-Atlantic Security and Cooperation 8ᵗʰ July 1997

Managing the International System over the Next Ten Years: A Report to the trilateral Commission, The Trilateral Commission New York, Paris and Tokyo, July 1997

Mandelbaum, Michael, *The Bush Foreign Policy*, Foreign Affairs, Vol. 70, No. 1 1991

Martin, Laurence, *The Global Century*, Chapter 27 Alliances and Alignments in a Globalization World, Institute for National Strategic Studies National Defense University, 2001

Maybaumwisniewski, Susan C. and Sommerville, Mary A., *Blue Horizon: United States-Japan-PRC Tripartite Relations, National Defense University*, 1997

Mearsheimer, John J., *Back to the Future: Instability in Europe After the Cold War*, International Security, Vol. 15 No. 1 (Summer 1990)

Michishita Narushige, *Alliance After Peace in Korea*, Survival Autumn 1999, The IISS Quarterly,

Miyaji Shinobu, *This is Yomiuri, 1999.2*

Mochizuki, Mike M., *Economics and Security: A Conceptual Framework*, The Council on Foreign Relations 1999

Mochizuki, Mike M., *Toward A True Alliance*, Brookings Institution Press, 1997

Modality of the Security and Defense Capability of Japan, Advisory Group on Defense Issues, August 12, 1994

Moreland, Ota, Pan'kov Captain, *Naval Cooperation in the Pacific: Looking to the Future*, Center for International Security and Arms Control in Stanford University, February 1993

Morgenthau, Hans J. Revised by Kenneth W. Thompson, *Politics Among Nations Brief Edition*, McGraw-Hill, Inc, 1993

National Defense Program Guideline for FY 2005 and After, Government of Japan, December 2004

National Security Strategy of the United States, Washington, DC, August 1991

National Security Strategy for a New Century, The White House, December 1999

National Security Strategy of the United States of America, The White House, September 2002

NATO-Russia Relations: A New Quality, Declaration by Heads of States and Government of NATO Member States and the Russian Federation, May 28, 2002

NATO's Strategic Concept, by the Heads of State and Governments Part II-Strategic Perspectives, The Evolving Strategic Environment, Paragraph 12, 1999

Nelsen, Harvey W., *Power and Insecurity: Beijing, Moscow, and Washington 1948–1988*, Boulder, CO. Lynn Rienner, 1989

New World Coming: American Security in the 21st century, The United States Commission on National Security 21st Century, September 15 1999

Niksch, Larry A., *CRS Report for Congress 96–798F Senkaku Islands Dispute: The US Legal Relationship and Obligations*, 1996

Nye, Joseph S., Jr., *The United States and East Asia: Working Together for a Secure Future*, July 1995

Nye, Joseph S., Jr., and Owens, William A., 'America's Information Edge', *Foreign Affairs*, Vol. 75, No. 2, March/April 1996

Osgood, Robert E., *Alliance and American Foreign Policy*, The Johns Hopkins Press, 1968

Piracy and Armed Robbery Against Ships Annual Report 1 January–31 December 1999, International Chamber of Commerce, International Maritime Bureau, January 2000

Political Platform of DPJ's Hatoyama Noted, FBIS-EAS-96-203, November 1, 1996

Proliferation: Threat and response, The US Department of Defense, January 2001

Prospects for Global Order, Royal Institute of International Affairs, London 1993

Przystup, James, *China, Japan, and the United States*, the Council on Foreign Relations, 1999

Quadrennial Defense Review Report, US Department of Defense, September 30, 2001

Rawski, Thomas, 'How cooked are the books?', *The Economist*, March 16, 2002

Reich, Robert B., *The Work of Nations*, Vintage Books, 1992

Risse-Kappen, Thomas, *Collective Identity in a Democratic Community: The Case of NATO, in The Culture of National Security*, Columbia University Press, 1996

Risse-Kappen, Thomas, *Cooperation Among democracies: The European Influence On US Foreign Policy*, Princeton University Press, 1995

ROK-US Security Consultative Meeting Joint Communiqué, November 1, 1996, Washington, DC

Roosevelt, Theodore, *The Awakening China, Outlook* 90, 28 November 1908

Rosecrance, Richard, *The Rise of the Trading State*, Basic Books, 1986

Ross, Robert S., *A New World: American Grand Strategy in the Post-Cold War Era*

Rubin, Robert, Testimony before the House Banking Committee on the Global Economy, September 16, 1998, and Summers Lawrence H., Testimony before the Senate Budget Committee, September 23, 1998

Rubinstein, Gregg A., *US–Japan Armaments Cooperation*, The Council on Foreign Relations, 1999

Rumsfeld, Secretary and Myers, Gen., *News Transcript*, United States Department of Defense, Monday, November 4, 2002

Rymer, Capt. E.H., to Admiralty, *Japan at War 1914–19*, Public Record Office, London, 11 March 1918

Samuels, Richard J. and Twomey, Christopher P., *The Eagle Eyes the Pacific: American Foreign Policy Options in East Asia after the Cold War*, The Council on Foreign Relations, 1999

Sassa Atsuyuki, *Politico-Military no susume*, Toshi Shuppan Kabushikigaisha, 1994

Secretary Rumsfeld Press Conference NATO Defense Ministerial, United States Department of Defense News Transcript, Friday, February 6, 2004, p. 4

Shibayama Futoshi, *Japan-US Defense Cooperation and the Road to Alliance Missile Defense (AMD), The journal of International Security*, Vol. 29, No. 4 (Mar. 2002)

Snyder, Glenn H., *The Security Dilemma in Alliance Politics*, Vol.36, July 1984

Spykman, Nicholas John, *America's Strategy in World Politics*, Institute of International Studies Yale University, 1942

Stackpole, Marine Corps Lieutenant General Henry C., referred in his famous interview while commanding the III Marine Expeditionary Force in 1989.

Statement on combating terrorism: Adapting the Alliance's Defense
   Capabilities, NATO Press Releases No. 2, December 18, 2001

Stone, Laura, *Whither Trade and Security? A Historical Perspective*,
   The Council on Foreign Relations 1999

Strategic Assessment, Institute for National Strategic Studies,
   National Defense University, 1998, 1999

Asahi Shinbun article dated September 19, 1998

*Testimony at Budget Hearing before the Senate Foreign Relations
   Committee*, US Department of States, February 5, 2002

Thucydides, *History of the Peloponnesian War*, Penguin Classics,
   1954

The Straits Times, April 5, 2004

*To Prevail – An American Strategy for the Campaign against
   Terrorism*, CSIS, November 2001

Treaty of Mutual Cooperation and Security Between Japan and
   US, June 23, 1960

Tucker, Robert, *A New Isolationism: Threat or Promise?*

Tyson, Laura D'Andrea, *Who's Bashing Whom?*, Institute for
   International Economics 1992

United States and Asia: Toward a New US Strategy and Force Posture,
   Rand Corporation, May 2001

United States and Japan: Advancing Toward a Mature Partnership,
   Institute for National Strategic Studies National Defense
   Studies, October 2000

United States Security Strategy for Europe and NATO, US Department
   of Defense, 1995

United States Security Strategy for the East Asia-Pacific Region, DOD-
   ISA Feb. 1995

United States Security Strategy for the East Asia-Pacific Region (EASR),
   Secretary of Defense, Nov. 1998

Walt, Stephen M., *The Origins of Alliance*, Cornell University
   Press, 1987

Waltz, Kenneth N., 'The Emerging Structure of International
   Politics', *International Security*, Vol. 18, No. 2, Fall 1993

Waltz, Kenneth N., *Theory of International Politics* Fifth Edition,
   McGraw-Hill, Inc., 1979

Watanabe Koji, *Japan in Need of Reform and Trilateralism*, The
   Trilateral Commission, July 1997

Weinberger, Caspar and Schweizer, Peter, *The Next War*, 1996

Wich, Richard, *Sino-Soviet Crisis Politics*, Council on East Asia
   Studies, Harvard University, 1980

Wolfowitz, Paul, *Managing Our Way To A Peaceful Century*, The Trilateral Commission, July 1997

Wolfowitz, Paul, *Speech at the 38th Munich Conference on Security Policy*, Remarks of Deputy Secretary, February 2, 2002

Wood, Lieutenant Commander I.D.H., Canadian Navy, *Piracy Is Deadlier Than Ever*, US Naval Institute Proceedings January 2000

Yahuda, Michael, *The International Politics of the Asia-Pacific, 1945–1995*, Routledge, 1996

Zoellick, Robert B., A Republican Foreign Policy, Foreign Affairs, January/February 2000

Index

Vice-Admiral (Retired) Fumio Ota
Director of the Center for Security and Crisis Management
Education, Japan National Defense Academy.